The Supreme Vocation of Women

Melissa Maleski

The Supreme Vocation of Women

According to St. John Paul II

SOPHIA INSTITUTE PRESS
Manchester, New Hampshire

Sophia Institute Press
Box 5284, Manchester, NH 03108
1-800-888-9344

www.SophiaInstitute.com

Sophia Institute Press® is a registered trademark of Sophia Institute.

Library of Congress Cataloging-in-Publication Data

Names: Maleski, Melissa, author.

Title: The supreme vocation of women : according to St. John Paul II / Melissa Maleski.

Description: Manchester, New Hampshire : Sophia Institute Press, 2020. | Includes bibliographical references. | Summary: "Explores the Catholic Church's consistent vision of womanhood as a powerful and vital agent for good throughout salvation history, and how that agency is challenged by the world's understanding of the nature and dignity of women"— Provided by publisher.

Identifiers: LCCN 2020003505 | ISBN 9781644130285 (paperback) | ISBN 9781644130292 (ebook)

Subjects: LCSH: Women in the Catholic Church. | Women—Religious aspects—Catholic Church.

Classification: LCC BX2347.8.W6 M353 2020 | DDC 233.082—dc23

LC record available at https://lccn.loc.gov/2020003505

First printing

*For the fierce, faith-filled, and fantastic women
of the Wormser, Nowell, and Maleski clans,
especially my daughter, Adele,
and my goddaughters Sara and Angelina.*

And for the men who love them.

Contents

The Supreme Vocation of Women

Introduction

In 2008, Luciano Garbati had a thought: *What if Medusa wasn't the real monster?* Inspired by this, he created a sculpture that flipped the classic myth on its head, allowing Medusa to keep hers. This new Medusa stands tall, naked, and unafraid of the observer's gaze. Her feet are firmly planted with the left foot slightly ahead of the right. Strong arms run parallel to an impressively athletic frame, terminating in hands that hold the elements of victory: a sword in her left and the head of her enemy in her right. The severed head of Perseus wears an expression of soft dismay, as if he realized in his last moment that his manhood was no match for a woman and it made him want to cry. The new Medusa's head combines her reputed mortal beauty and the cursed serpentine locks. The snakes are well coiffed, draping attractively over one shoulder. Medusa's face is beautiful but set in a mask of stony determination. No joy or relief radiates from her gaze. She stares straight ahead, grimly prepared for the next head that needs to roll.

What makes the new Medusa so arresting is the palpability of her wrath. It permeates her frame and pours from her eyes, and you cannot help but feel the burn. Her wrath is familiar to many,[1] for it is the wrath of oppressed womanhood.

More than just an expression of rage, the new Medusa personifies the spirit of feminist activism that has steadily influenced society for the last 175 years. Her head and body, traditionally weaponized by forces outside her control, are now completely her own; symbols of the fight for the right to vote, economic rights, reproductive rights, and sexual freedom. Her gaze is fixed, and her weapon is sharp; women will no longer accept anything less than the same political, social, and cultural privileges that men enjoy. The new Medusa has had enough of institutional sexism, and she cannot — will not — rest until she has won back what was stolen from her: her own self.

One institution in the new Medusa's crosshairs is the Catholic Church. In the October 2018 edition of *Women Church World*, the French biblical scholar Anne-Marie Pelletier lamented that all women faithful, religious and lay alike, "know all too well the haughty, condescending, disdainful gaze turned their way and the daily experience of obedience imposed by men who jealously hold for themselves the prestige of knowledge and authority." The magazine's editor, Lucetta Scaraffia, echoed the sentiment while calling for an increase in female leadership in the Church:

> It is true that women, even the most obedient, do not truly feel part of the church, but at most (they feel like) obedient daughters.... If they did feel they were a welcome part, then they would fight no matter what their

---

[1] Annaliese Griffin, "The Story behind the Medusa Statue That Has Become the Perfect Avatar for Women's Rage," Quartz, October 3, 2018, https://qz.com/quartzy/1408600/the-medusa-statue-that-became-a-symbol-of-feminist-rage/.

role "with all the weapons they possess, which are not trivial things." ... The condition of women in the church will change only if women have the courage to begin to change things from below, with denunciations if necessary, with questions that are never asked."[2]

Neither Pelletier nor Scaraffia speak for all women, as they imply, but they do echo a particular frustration of many women—and men. People have this notion that the Church is an archaic patriarchy that neither understands nor likes women. Those who hold such a notion usually cite two things as proof: little nuggets of misogyny, adapted from Greek philosophy, that are sprinkled throughout early Church writings, and an unyielding adherence to certain doctrines that are intimately tied to women.

Aristotle, whose philosophy and ethical principles were found to be the most compatible with divine revelation, confessed that while women were more equal to men than slaves or children were, there was still a natural and insurmountable hierarchy between the sexes:

> For although there may be exceptions to the order of nature, the male is by nature fitter for command than the female, just as the elder and full-grown is superior to the younger and more immature. But in most constitutional states the citizens rule and are ruled by turns, for the idea of a constitutional state implies that the natures of the citizens are equal, and do not differ at all. Nevertheless,

---

[2] Quoted in Carol Glatz, "Women Must Fight Clericalism to Heal Church, Vatican Publication Says," CatholicPhilly.com, October 1, 2018, http://catholicphilly.com/2018/10/news/world-news/women-must-fight-clericalism-to-heal-church-vatican-publication-says/.

when one rules and the other is ruled we endeavor to create a difference of outward forms and names and titles of respect.... The relation of the male to the female is of this kind, but there the inequality is permanent.[3]

Almost 1,700 years later, the writings of St. Thomas Aquinas indicate that the Church did not appear to have deviated far from Aristotle on this point. In his *Summa Theologica*, St. Thomas explains the creation of woman this way:

It was necessary for woman to be made, as the Scripture says, as a "helper" to man; not, indeed, as a helpmate in other works, as some say, since man can be more efficiently helped by another man in other works; but as a helper in the work of generation.... As regards to the individual nature, woman is defective and misbegotten.... On the other hand, as regards human nature in general, woman is not misbegotten, but is included in nature's intention as directed to the work of generation.[4]

He does add, not long after saying this, that there is an equality of sorts between man and woman. The proof is in the symbolism of woman being made from Adam's rib:

I answer that it was right for the woman to be made from the rib of a man. First, to signify the social union of man and woman, for the woman should neither "use authority over man," and so she was not made from his head; nor was it right for her to be subject to man's contempt as his slave, and so she was not made from

---

[3] Aristotle, *Politics*, bk. 1, chap. 12.
[4] Thomas Aquinas, *Summa Theologica*, I, q. 92.

his feet. Secondly, for the sacramental signification; for from the side of Christ sleeping on the Cross the Sacraments flowed—namely, blood and water—on which the Church was established.[5]

In between Aristotle and Aquinas were others. St. Augustine adhered to Aristotle's position, marking him as a median between the Philosopher and St. Thomas.[6] Tertullian called women "the devil's gateway" and blamed the death of the Son of God on the female sex.[7] St. John Chrysostom espoused the idea that God made men to look after the more important and necessary things in life, such as civil governance, while women were made to look after the inferior, but still honorable, tasks of running the household and raising children.[8] St. Clement of Alexandria warned women to consume alcohol slowly and gracefully since their nature was more prone to licentiousness.[9] And St. Gregory the Great commended women who withheld themselves from Holy Communion while menstruating because, while not a sin in and of itself, it is a consequence of Original Sin and a reminder of fallen feminine nature.[10]

---

[5] Ibid., answer to obj. 3.

[6] Augustine, "The Literal Meaning of Genesis," trans. John Hammond Taylor, S.J., *Ancient Christian Writers* (New York: Newman Press, 1982), vol. 2, bk. 9, chap. 5.

[7] Tertullian, *On the Apparel of Women*, bk. 1, chap. 1.

[8] John Chrysostom, "How to Choose a Wife," *On Marriage and Family Life*, trans. Catherine P. Roth and David Anderson (New York: St. Vladimir's Press, 1986), 97.

[9] Clement of Alexandria, *Paedagogus*, bk. 2, chap. 2.

[10] Gregory the Great, Epistle LXIV, answer to Augustine's tenth question, *Nicene and Post-Nicene Fathers*, 2nd series, vol. 13, *Gregory the Great, Ephraim Syrus, Aphrahat*, ed. Philip Schaff and

The Supreme Vocation of Women

On the surface, it is hard conclusively to confirm or deny how influential these small thoughts were in the Church's theological and pastoral understanding of womanhood up until modernity. There is no documented chain of discussions that argue for or against the theological or pastoral merits of such ideas about women. The Church was elsewhere occupied; heresies, schisms, and general societal shifts in ideology and technological advancement required urgent attention. But when the Church did begin to attend to the pressing questions surrounding womanhood, almost seven hundred years after St. Thomas Aquinas lived and wrote, the hopeful anticipation of a monumental shift in how the Church understood and communicated Catholic doctrine on women's issues proved that these statements had some kind of lingering effect on the faithful.

The Second Vatican Council (1962–1965) was called to examine how the Church could communicate her timeless truths to a rapidly changing society. For the first time, the specific role of women was addressed head-on in this communication. According to Sr. Mary Luke Tobin, one of fifteen female auditors at the council, the results were "just a tiny crack in the door, to a recognition of the vast indifference toward women and the ignoring of their potential within the whole body of the church."[11] Twenty years after the close of the council, the national board of the Leadership Council of Women Religious (LCWR) enumerated many of the

---

Henry Wace (Grand Rapids: Wm. B. Eerdmans, 1973), http://www.tertullian.org/fathers2/NPNF2-13/Npnf2-13-06.htm#P959_381185.

[11] Mary Luke Tobin, "Women in the Church Since Vatican II," *America*, November 1, 1986, https://www.americamagazine.org/issue/100/women-church-vatican-ii.

ways that the Church continues to treat women with prejudice: patriarchy, nominal female participation in liturgical worship, sexist humor, female exclusion from Church governance, the heavier burden placed on women by the doctrines on artificial contraception, abortion, and sterilization, and a lack of public support for civil legislation that empowers women.[12] The LCWR's litany of criticism is the same critical refrain today, more than thirty years after its composition.

No wonder the new Medusa has her eyes on the Church. The evidence presented so far appears damning. But there is so much more to the story of the Church's stance on women that is absent from this scant evidence. In a twist of pure irony, it is the reimagined Medusa herself that starts us on the journey to the truth. For the transformation from vanquished monster to victorious warrior against oppression and denigration has made the new Medusa look almost exactly like a nineteenth-century depiction of Judith, the biblical widow who saved Israel by beheading the Assyrian general Holofernes. In 1840, August Riedel painted a portrait of Judith with the head of Holofernes in one hand and a sword in the other. Judith, like the new Medusa, stands tall and unafraid, but she is neither tense nor naked. Her body is not her message, but you get the sense that her essence is communicated in her clothing: a pure white cloth draped around her frame, bound up in a resplendent crimson and gold skirt sash. Her right hand holds Holofernes's head slightly behind her body, turning his face away from observation, and her left rests on the hilt of her sword, which is planted forward and away from her body. Her beautiful face is turned to the side, her gaze calmly fixed on something distant and ephemeral, as if she is in peaceful contemplation.

---

[12] Ibid.

The Supreme Vocation of Women

Engaging in a detailed comparison of the two depictions of feminine strength and agency merits its own theological reflection, but it is beyond the scope of this book. For our purposes, it suffices to say that Judith was a woman of incredible agency, and her story never needed to be reimagined to make her so. She simply was, and she was immortalized in Scripture for it. And she is not alone. A number of women are prominently acknowledged in both the Old and New Testaments. There is Deborah, the lone female in the line of Old Testament judges, and there is Queen Esther. We also see faithful Ruth, contrite Mary and her industrious sister, Martha, and the sick woman who dared all social convention to touch the hem of Jesus' garment. And there is the Blessed Virgin Mary, the woman who encompasses all that God intended to communicate through feminine humanity. Catholic Tradition also recognizes many women as saints for their heroic agency and positive influence on both the Church and the world. In addition to the hundreds of women who are feasted and memorialized throughout the liturgical year, we recall the early female martyrs during the prayers said at Mass, and we have four women who are honored as Doctors of the Church: Sts. Teresa of Avila, Catherine of Siena, Thérèse of Lisieux, and Hildegard of Bingen.

These women are remarkable in their own right, but the Church does not honor and venerate them, or the hundreds of other women like them, because they were women who simply did or said something. The Church has recognized in these women the living witness of divine revelation and earmarked them for future generations to reflect on, learn from, and ask the intercession of. These women have, in past generations, inspired *both women and men* to have greater faith in the Church, to be obedient to the will of God, and to give generously of themselves in the service of growing, protecting, and sharing the richness of the Catholic Faith through good governance, education, and caring for the sick and those in need. For our generation, these women are that and more: they are a mosaic, coming together as a united sisterhood to exhibit what the Church actually professes about the nature and agency of womanhood. Together, they stand as a compelling counterargument to the notion that the Church is oppressively patriarchal.

In the pages that follow, this mosaic of womanhood will be woven into the explosive growth of the Church's written reflections on the nature and agency of women in the Church and the world since the Second Vatican Council, especially the seminal works of Pope St. John Paul II. These documents, with their combined force, offer a new perspective on the Church's consistent profession of the equal dignity and agency of women and men throughout salvation history and explore the ways that the faithful can more fully apply the Church's convictions to their agency as Christian witnesses. The new Medusa is strong, but as we will see, she is but a pale imitation of the empowered womanhood that the world desperately wishes to see validated.

1

Enigmatic Last Words

Everyone, including the Holy Father himself, knew that the first of the Last Things was not far from Pope John Paul II on that warm August day in Lourdes. The pilgrims, the reporters, and the world were transfixed by the ailing pontiff, but John Paul II had one thing on his mind: Mary. It was well known that John Paul II credited the Blessed Mother's intercession for his surviving an assassination attempt in 1981; his pontificate since that time was imbued with his deep gratitude and devotion to her.

Despite death's impending arrival, the 150th anniversary of Mary's visitation to Bernadette Soubirous was not an event that John Paul II was going to let pass by without presenting himself at the famous grotto to offer his due veneration and exhortation:

> By her words and her silence the Virgin Mary stands before us as a model for our pilgrim way. *It is not an easy way*: as a result of the fall of our first parents, humanity is marked by the wounds of sin, whose consequences continue to be felt also among the redeemed. But evil and death *will not have the last word!* Mary confirms this

by her whole life, for she is a *living witness of the victory of Christ, our Passover.*[13]

As he had done many times before, the Holy Father used the Blessed Mother's witness to direct the faithful in their own:

Listen to her, *young people* who seek an answer capable of giving meaning to your lives.... From this grotto I issue a special call to *women*. Appearing here, Mary entrusted her message *to a young girl*, as if to emphasize *the special mission of women* in our own time, tempted as it is by materialism and secularism: to be in today's society *a witness of those essential values* which are seen only with the eyes of the heart. To you, women, falls the task of being *sentinels of the Invisible!* I appeal urgently to all of you, dear brothers and sisters, to do everything in your power to ensure that life, each and every life, will be respected from conception to its natural end.... *Be men and women of freedom!* But remember: human freedom is a freedom wounded by sin. It is a freedom which itself needs to be set free. *Christ is its liberator*; he is the one who "for freedom has set us free" (cf. Gal. 5:1). Defend that freedom![14]

This was a familiar refrain from John Paul II. During his pontificate, the Holy Father wrote and spoke often on topics relating to respect for life, marriage and family issues, and the dignity of the sexes. Preferring to focus on the spectacle of "God's athlete" slowly and publicly succumbing to unimaginable suffering, news outlets made only perfunctory acknowledgments

[13] John Paul II, Homily at Lourdes (August 15, 2004), no. 5.
[14] Ibid., no. 7.

of the content of the pope's homily. Even the *National Catholic Reporter's* John L. Allen Jr. could not resist the temptation to focus on the circumstances and implications surrounding John Paul II's visit rather than on his message.[15] It is understandable, then, that the appearance of a brand-new turn of phrase in the pope's homily — "sentinels of the Invisible" — went largely unnoticed.

Key Works by John Paul II

It may be understandable, but it is still a bit curious. Over his twenty-seven-year papacy, John Paul II imparted an unprecedented and coherent theological and anthropological understanding of the human person that is recognizable in every modern document that touches on, however briefly, the subjects of human sexuality, the family, and the dignity of women. His works significantly influenced how the Church of the third millennium reflects on and responds to society's evolving views on the subject.[16] Of these, the following are of primary importance: *Theology of the Body, Familiaris Consortio, Redemptoris Mater, Mulieris Dignitatem,* and *Christifideles Laici.*

Theology of the Body (1979–1984)

Theology of the Body was a revolutionary theological reflection on human sexuality. Throughout 129 lectures, John Paul II managed

---

[15] See John L. Allen Jr., "The Pope in Lourdes: Is Too Much Hope a Dangerous Thing?," *National Catholic Reporter*, August 16, 2004, http://www.nationalcatholicreporter.org/update/nt081604.htm.

[16] Congregation for the Doctrine of the Faith, *Letter to the Bishops of the Catholic Church on the Collaboration of Men and Women in the Church and in the World* (May 31, 2004), no. 1.

to present a comprehensive anthropology of the human person that balanced the physical, psychological, and ontological dignity of both sexes with uncompromised integrity. John Paul II breathed new life into the Genesis accounts of Creation, making the most familiar of Bible stories feel as if it were being read for the first time. Jesus' exhortation to return to "the beginning" in regard to the laws of marriage (Matt. 19:4) and the critical text of Ephesians 5 are given greater contextual depth. In *Theology of the Body*, John Paul II also gave the Church a distinct vocabulary with his anthropology: the "sincere gift of self," "mutual gift," "reciprocal knowledge," and the "language of the body" being the most widely recognized.

Familiaris Consortio (1981)

Known for the exhortation "Family, become what you are," *Familiaris Consortio* is the first of John Paul II's writings to address the value and role of Christian marriage and family. Written while giving the lecture series that would become *Theology of the Body*, the document mirrors and further develops much of what the lectures already introduced: "reciprocal knowledge," mutual or reciprocal "gift," and what it means to get back to "the beginning." John Paul II also considered the equal dignity of men and women and the subsequent justice of women's active presence in public life.

Redemptoris Mater (1987)

The encyclical *Redemptoris Mater* contemplates the Blessed Mother and her role in salvation history. John Paul II did not directly address the dignity of women, but he did make plain his intention to further the Church's understanding of womanhood through the Mother of God:

This Marian dimension of Christian life takes on special importance in relation to women and their status. In fact, femininity has a unique relationship with the Mother of the Redeemer, a subject which can be studied in greater depth elsewhere. Here I simply wish to note that the figure of Mary of Nazareth sheds light on womanhood as such by the very fact that God, in the sublime event of the Incarnation of his Son, entrusted himself to the ministry, the free and active ministry of a woman. It can thus be said that women, by looking to Mary, find in her the secret of living their femininity with dignity and of achieving their own true advancement.[17]

Mulieris Dignitatem (1988)

Mulieris Dignitatem was John Paul II's response to a request by the 1987 synod of bishops "for a further study of the anthropological and theological bases that are needed in order to solve the problems connected with the meaning and dignity of being a woman and being a man ... of understanding the reason for and the consequences of the Creator's decision that the human being should always and only exist as a woman or a man."[18] The apostolic letter delivered a resounding affirmation of what the pope called the "feminine genius."

Christifideles Laici (1988)

In *Christifideles Laici*, a general exhortation on the vocation and mission of lay faithful, John Paul II devoted a significant portion

[17] John Paul II, *Redemptoris Mater* (March 25, 1987), no. 46.
[18] John Paul II, apostolic letter *Mulieris Dignitatem* (August 15, 1988), 1.

of the document to promoting the authentic dignity of women in the Church and the world:

> If anyone has this task of advancing the dignity of women in the Church and society, it is women themselves, who must recognize their responsibility as leading characters. There is still much effort to be done, in many parts of the world and in various surroundings, to destroy that unjust and deleterious mentality which considers the human being as a thing, as an object to buy and sell, as an instrument for selfish interests or for pleasure only. Women themselves, for the most part, are the prime victims of such a mentality.[19]

John Paul II also expressed concern for preserving "the role of the family in its task of being the *primary place of 'humanization'* for the person and society."[20]

All of John Paul II's other documents that include a discussion of human sexuality and the dignity of women repeat and reinforce the theological developments he formulated during the first third of his papacy. The 1993 encyclical *Veritatis Splendor* references *Familiaris Consortio* twice. *Theology of the Body* echoes throughout his 1994 *Letter to Families*. A year later, John Paul II incorporated *Familiaris Consortio, Letter to Families*, and *Mulieris Dignitatem* into the encyclical *Evangelium Vitae*.

That same year he also wrote two separate letters: *Letter to Women* and *Letter to Mrs. Gertrude Mongella, Secretary General of the Fourth World Conference on Women of the United Nations*. In the

---

[19] John Paul II, post-synodal apostolic exhortation *Christifideles Laici* (December 30, 1988), no. 49.

[20] Ibid., no. 40.

first, he hearkened back to *Mulieris Dignitatem* by encouraging the faithful to more deeply reflect on the feminine genius to "bring out the full truth about women."[21] In the second, he drew from the language of *Christifideles Laici* to ask the secretary-general to present an authentic vision of womanhood to the world: "It should in fact be clear that 'when women are able fully to share their gifts with the whole community, the very way in which society understands and organizes itself is improved.' ... This is a recognition of *the unique role which women have in humanizing society* and directing it towards the positive goals of solidarity and peace."[22]

John Paul II did not publish much after the mid-1990s on the topics of human sexuality and the dignity of women. His reverence for and devotion to Mary, so eloquently expounded on in *Redemptoris Mater*, remained an explicit facet of his writings and speeches, but the final third of his papacy did not significantly contribute to the Church's ongoing reflections. That task was readily taken up by professional theologians and the general laity.[23] It is truly curious, then, that when John Paul II revisited feminine dignity in his homily at Lourdes, he appeared to go a little off script: "To you, women, falls the task of being *sentinels of the Invisible!*"

We will never know for sure what John Paul II intended to communicate when he introduced that phrase. It is possible that

---

[21] John Paul II, *Letter to Women* (June 29, 1995), no. 12.

[22] John Paul II, *Letter to Mrs. Gertrude Mongella, Secretary General of the Fourth World Conference on Women of the United Nations* (May 26, 1995), no. 5.

[23] *Mulieris Dignitatem* sparked a vast interest in the "feminine genius," and much of the lay scholarship that followed the document's publication focuses on a theological and practical understanding of the concept's meaning. A quick Google search of "feminine genius" (as of early 2019) pulls 47,700,000 results to peruse.

he had chosen a new way to summarize certain elements of his theological anthropology. It is also possible that John Paul II knew the Church would be steering through uncharted waters in the coming decades and pointed the way forward one final time. What we can say for sure is that this unique commission was not an accident or an empty platitude. John Paul II was communicating something profound and important, not only to women but to the whole world. Looking back through his legacy and the deposit of faith that he drew upon, we can synthesize the meaning and value of "sentinels of the Invisible" for the Church and the world.

"Sentinels of the Invisible"

"Sentinels of the Invisible" is a powerful phrase. But what does it mean? According to the *Merriam-Webster Dictionary*, a sentinel is a person who stands guard or watch, "especially a soldier standing guard at a point of passage"; and "invisible" means "incapable by nature of being seen: not perceptible by vision; inaccessible to view." John Paul II never wrote with a flair for the dramatic. Even his plays, such as *The Jeweler's Shop*, are deliberate and unpretentious meditations. We can safely assume that John Paul II chose the words "sentinels of the Invisible" carefully and intended them to be understood as close to their literal meaning as possible.

On the surface, it seems easier to begin with the word "sentinel." It is not difficult to imagine a woman who stands guard: the mother who watches over her small child as he sleeps, or the wife who keeps vigil at the hospital bedside of her ailing husband. The image of women as soldiers is on the rise as well, thanks to changing policies in many first-world countries. But without a firm understanding of the invisible things that women are tasked with guarding—specifically as women—the term "sentinel" can't be fully realized. Let's begin with understanding the word "Invisible" as John Paul II intended. "Invisible" is capitalized in the homily's text, indicating that it is a proper noun. Further, we are meant to understand it as a *who*, not a *what*. John Paul II communicated this word in the same way that the Church traditionally capitalizes words such as "Church," "Blessed Virgin," "Holy Spirit," and "Son."

Who is *the Invisible?* God is! But this answer should not be taken for granted on its own. Catholic theology explicitly states that God is not only a unique and living being—He is life itself. Though it is acclaimed in the Catholic creeds and solemnly celebrated in the Sacrifice of the Mass, most Christians struggle fully to understand God as more than an idea or a spirit that inhabits the living things of the world. All things, visible and invisible, have their beginning in God; He existed before our idea of Him did. This is an ancient teaching of the Church. St. Thomas Aquinas saw fit to give a straight account of this doctrine with the words of St. Augustine: "The trace of the Trinity appears in creatures."[24]

Inseparable from this teaching is that man is made in the image and likeness of God and therefore bears the dignity and responsibility of giving witness to that image in the world. John Paul II's *Theology of the Body* was revolutionary precisely because it was the first time a pope had ever attempted explicitly to identify what the "trace of the Trinity" *looks like* in the highest of God's creation: man as male and female. It laid the foundation for a theological and anthropological explanation of what is universally true for all humans, so that a clearer understanding

---

[24] *Summa Theologica*, I, q. 45, art. 7.

of what makes male and female truly unique—what the Church calls "complementarity of the sexes"—could be well articulated. Complementarity and its implications for our understanding of the meaning of "sentinels of the Invisible" will be explored in depth in the next chapter, but at present it suffices to say that the concept conveys the divine truth that women have a specific way of expressing the image and likeness of God. This way is of equal importance and equal dignity to the way of men.

Since God is completely immaterial, which of His attributes make up the image we male and female humans are created in? One answer might seem to be all of them! But there are certain attributes of God that mankind simply does not have: omniscience and omnipotence are two. Being outside the bounds of time is another. Limited as we are by our nature as created beings, the Church recognizes that mankind has certain qualities that, through the use of natural reason and divine revelation, reveal themselves to be a veiled imitation of God: the attributes of love, truth, and goodness, which flow from the human soul's unique character. As the *Catechism of the Catholic Church* explains, "Endowed with a spiritual soul, with intellect and with free will, the human person is from his very conception ordered to God and destined for eternal beatitude. He pursues his perfection in 'seeking and loving what is true and good' (GS 15 § 2)" (1711). St. John touches on this truth and goodness as he explains that God is love:

> He who does not love does not know God; for God is love. In this the love of God was made manifest among us, that God sent his only Son into the world, so that we might live through him. In this is love, not that we loved God but that he loved us and sent his Son to be the expiation for our sins. Beloved, if God so loved us, we also

ought to love one another. No man has ever seen God; if we love one another, God abides in us and his love is perfected in us.

By this we know that we abide in him and he in us, because he has given us of his own Spirit. And we have seen and testify that the Father has sent his Son as the Savior of the world. Whoever confesses that Jesus is the Son of God, God abides in him, and he in God. So we know and believe the love God has for us. God is love, and he who abides in love abides in God, and God abides in him. In this is love perfected with us, that we may have confidence for the day of judgment, because as he is so are we in this world. There is no fear in love, but perfect love casts out fear. For fear has to do with punishment, and he who fears is not perfected in love. We love, because he first loved us. If any one says, "I love God," and hates his brother, he is a liar; for he who does not love his brother whom he has seen, cannot love God whom he has not seen. (1 John 4:8–20)

To "abide" in God, according to St. John, we must love God, confess the truth about His Son and the Spirit, and act in goodness toward our brother. We must do as God first does.

John Paul II echoed this in his work, emphasizing the primacy of love as St. John did. In *Familiaris Consortio*, he said, "God inscribed in the humanity of man and woman the vocation, and thus the capacity and responsibility, of love and communion" (11). He explained further in *Mulieris Dignitatem*:

Love is an ontological and ethical requirement of the person. The person must be loved, since love alone corresponds to what the person is. This explains *the commandment of love*, known already in the Old Testament (cf. Deut. 6:5; Lev. 19:18) and placed by Christ at the very center of the Gospel "*ethos*" (cf. Matt. 22:36–40; Mark 12:28–34). This also explains the *primacy of love* expressed by Saint Paul in the First Letter to the Corinthians: "the greatest of these is love" (cf. 13:13). (29)

Mankind, as male and female, are equally tasked with revealing and returning God's love, the truth of who He is, and the goodness that is proper to all of His works.

Without reducing the inherent dignity and responsibility of men to live out this human vocation, John Paul II felt that women had the special task of standing sentinel for God and the likeness of Himself that He infused in every human person. With more of an understanding of who—not what!—the *Invisible* is, we are one step closer to understanding what John Paul II believed womanhood was, by design, tasked with in the divine plan.

We can also conclude from this, and the Church's enduring teaching on human sexuality and the dignity of women, that John Paul II believed that women were not just persons who stood watch over the invisible God but that they were soldiers who stood at the very passage between God and His likeness in mankind:

> The moral and spiritual strength of a woman is joined to her awareness that *God entrusts the human being to her in a special way*. Of course, God entrusts every human being to each and every other human being. But this entrusting concerns women in a special way—precisely by reason of their femininity—and this in a particular way determines their vocation. The moral force of women, which draws strength from this awareness and this entrusting, expresses

itself in a great number of figures of the Old Testament, of the time of Christ, and of later ages right up to our own day. *A woman is strong because of her awareness of this entrusting*, strong because of the fact that God "entrusts the human being to her," always and in every way, even in the situations of social discrimination in which she may find herself.[25]

To John Paul II, women are truly and unambiguously *sentinels*.

[25] *Mulieris Dignitatem*, no. 30.

2

A Trace of the Trinity

Betty Friedan touched a nerve in 1960 when she declared that "women are people, too!"[26] This sentiment gave a public voice to the disaffection many women were feeling at being stuck in the traditional roles of wife and mother and the secret desire to break free from the captivity of societal norms to prioritize self-fulfillment. Three years later, Friedan published *The Feminine Mystique*, kicking off a new era of liberated womanhood. As revolutionary as her declaration seemed at the time, it does not match the seismic departure from conventional wisdom that happened when Christ preached the truth of women's full humanity — two thousand years earlier.

Though the memory of it has long faded into myth, the nascent Christian Faith took the unprecedented step of professing the inviolable dignity of women as human persons to the world. Not only women, but every person, regardless of age, sex, ethnicity, or station in life, had equal dignity in the eyes of God. St. Paul, taking his cue from Christ and the apostles, posited the first

---

[26] Betty Friedan, "Women Are People, Too!," *Good Housekeeping* (1960), https://www.goodhousekeeping.com/life/career/advice/a18890/1960-betty-friedan-article/.

pastoral applications of a universal inherent human dignity. He recommended that men who owned slaves "treat [them] justly and fairly, knowing that you also have a Master in heaven (Col. 4:1)," and that husbands should "love [their] wives, as Christ loved the church and gave himself up for her" (Eph. 5:25). This presumption of human dignity, which we now take for granted in the third millennium, shook the ancient world with its novelty and rankled as many people as it enticed to convert. The New Testament recounts a number of instances in which the Pharisees make plain their surprise at and discomfort with Jesus' inclusivity.[27] The Greek philosopher Celsus codified the pagan objections to Christianity with oozing disdain:

> What is said by a few who are considered as Christians, concerning the doctrine of Jesus and the precepts of Christianity, is not designed for the wiser, but for the more unlearned and ignorant part of mankind. For the following are their precepts: "Let no one who is erudite accede to us, no one who is wise, no one who is prudent … but let anyone who is unlearned, who is stupid, who is an infant in understanding boldly come to us." For the Christians openly acknowledge that such a one as these are worthy to be noticed by their God; manifesting by this, that they alone wish and are able to persuade the ignoble, the insensate, slaves, stupid women, and little children and fools.[28]

---

[27] See Matt. 9:11; Mark 2:16; Luke 5:30; 7:36–50; 15:2.
[28] "The Arguments of Celsus against the Christians," in *Arguments of Celsus, Porphyry, and the Emperor Julian, against the Christians,* ed. Thomas Taylor (London, 1830; Project Gutenberg, 2013),

The Church's presumption of, and concern for, the dignity and value of the human person was lived long before it was formally articulated. As early as A.D. 200, the Church advocated for a woman's right to choose her husband and to reject marriage altogether in favor of religious life. Christians were freeing slaves as early as the third century, popes were formally condemning forms of slavery as early as 1435,[29] and the Church was at the forefront of the modern social justice movement with the 1891 encyclical *Rerum Novarum*.

John Paul II's body of work on the dignity of the human person, especially that of women, assumes and continues the Church's enduring stance that "women are people, too." What sets John Paul II apart in his communication of this truth is his use of the philosophical system known as *personalism* to organize and systematically explain the Church's beliefs without sacrificing any theological integrity.

Personalism

Personalism was formally introduced in 1799 by the German Friedrich Schleiermacher. It reached America by 1863 and was introduced to the French by 1903. As a general discipline, it "emphasizes the significance, uniqueness, and inviolability of the person, as well as the person's essentially relational or social dimension.... [It is] any school of thought that focuses on the centrality of persons and their unique status among beings

---

19–20, https://www.gutenberg.org/files/37696/37696-h/37696-h.htm.

[29] Fr. Joel S. Panzer, *The Popes and Slavery* (New York: Alba House, 1996), 75–78.

in general."[30] A number of prominent Catholics, such as Dietrich von Hildebrand and Edith Stein, were applying a form of personalism to gender theory as early as the 1920s and 1930s, respectively. Before Stein entered the religious life as a Carmelite, she spent time in the company of Jacques Maritain, who, with Emmanuel Mounier and a few other Catholic philosophers, penned *The Personalist Manifesto*; not long after, in 1936, Mounier published an article called "Woman Is Also a Person."[31] Ten years later, Mounier lectured at a seminary in Krakow, Poland. One of the seminarians who heard Mounier speak was Karol Wojtyla, the future Pope John Paul II.

Wojtyla was equally impressed by the personalist tendencies of the German philosopher Max Scheler (1874–1928) and the sixteenth-century Catholic mystic St. John of the Cross. Scheler's perspective on ethics was instrumental in helping Wojtyla parse Immanuel Kant's ethical considerations of the person into what aligns with, and contradicts, Catholic theology.[32] In the early years of World War II, while hiding underground in Poland, he became acquainted with the works of St. John of the Cross. "To him I owe so much in my spiritual formation,"[33] John Paul II later

[30] Thomas D. Williams and Jan Olof Bengtsson, "Personalism," *Stanford Encyclopedia of Philosophy* (Spring 2020 edition), article published November 12, 2009; revised May 11, 2018.

[31] Prudence Allen, R.S.M., "Man-Woman Complementarity: The Catholic Inspiration," *Logos* 9, no. 3 (Summer 2006): 94, http://www.laity.va/content/dam/laici/documenti/donna/filosofia/english/man-woman-complementary-the-catholic-inspiration.pdf.

[32] Michael Waldstein, introduction to *Man and Woman He Created Them: A Theology of the Body*, by John Paul II (Boston: Pauline Books and Media, 2006), 36.

[33] *Theology of the Body*, 26.

said of the saint and his works. St. John of the Cross was the subject of Fr. Wojtyla's doctoral thesis in 1948, and his *Spiritual Canticle* was discussed in detail. All of St. John of the Cross's work profoundly affected the life and work of John Paul II, but three ideas found in the *Spiritual Canticle* resound throughout John Paul II's legacy: love and the cycle of mutual giving, the fittingness of the marriage analogy across all Christian experiences, and the root of love in the trinitarian image of the relationships between God the Father, God the Son, and God the Holy Spirit.[34]

Like von Hildebrand and Stein before him, John Paul II began his ethical considerations of the human person with the spiritual, pastoral, and anthropological relationship between the sexes. When he was still Karol Wojtyla, he published his first book, *Love and Responsibility*, in 1960. In it he said, "The body, and it alone, is capable of making visible what is invisible: the spiritual and divine."[35] By the time Wojtyla became Pope John Paul II and began his weekly lectures on the theology of the body, he had laid the foundation for a comprehensive theological and philosophical understanding of the human person by making significant contributions to the Second Vatican Council documents *Dignitatis Humanae* (Decree on Religious Freedom) and *Gaudium et Spes* (Pastoral Constitution on the Church in the Modern World). But with *Theology of the Body*, John Paul II unleashed the full force of his thought on the ethical dimensions of the human person.

---

[34] Ibid., 29–32.
[35] Fr. Karol Wojtyla, *Love and Responsibility*, trans. H. T. Willetts, (London: William Collins Sons, 1960; repr., San Francisco: Ignatius Press, 1993).

The Supreme Vocation of Women

Personalism and Theology of the Body

Most commonly used as a platform to evangelize engaged and married couples on the Church's teachings on sexual morality, *Theology of the Body* could be dismissed as a long-form "sex talk" (you know, the kind that very few people want to have). But although the goal of *Theology of the Body* is a defense of the traditional positions on marriage, chastity, celibacy, virginity, and the proscription on contraception, its purpose is to come to a deeper understanding of the human person, *simply as a person!* This is why, heeding Christ's "appeal to the beginning," John Paul II began his theology of the body with a series of reflections on man's creation. First, Adam (in Hebrew, "humanity") is created as "a body among bodies." He is placed among the living creatures of the world; in the process of naming them, he comes to a relative understanding of himself. Adam knows that he is alone in the world—there is no other creature quite like him. Then God pulls Adam back into the "moment before creation" by putting him into a deep sleep. Humanity reemerges as male and female: two distinct and complementary ways of being a human person. Only then does Adam fully understand his (and her!) humanity: "This at last is bone of my bones and flesh of my flesh; she shall be called Woman, because she was taken out of Man" (Gen. 2:23).

John Paul II's contemplative journey through man's creation provides us with a profound, if somewhat nebulous, first glimpse into the original nature of the human person. This nature, created "in the image of God" (Gen 1:27), is both capable of and responsible for making the invisible likeness of God visible in the world. From this, he concludes that the human person is unique among creatures; is capable of self-knowledge; relates to others;

through relationship with others, reflects the image of God; has two ways of being, male and female, that mutually enrich each other.[36] In conjunction with St. John's understanding that "God is love," John Paul II drew these further conclusions about the human person:

- Love is the "fundamental and innate vocation of the human being."[37]
- The relationship between persons is a "gift of self."
- Through the gift of self, we specifically reflect the trinitarian communion of Persons.
- Male and female are equal in created dignity but express that dignity distinctly.
- Humanity is understood only through the complementary expressions of male and female.

After making this initial sketch of the human person and male-female sexuality, John Paul II moved *Theology of the Body* along its expected trajectory into Christian doctrine and sexual morality.

We are accustomed to thinking and speaking along *Theology of the Body*'s trajectory, with good reason. There is an urgent need for the Church and the world to hear the truth that *Theology of the Body* leads us back to. But, we must admit, rarely do we have coffee shop–level conversations about the human person and sexuality that are not bound up, in some way, with the sexual act. And since we are here to discuss the meaning of women as sentinels of the Invisible, a moniker that seems to transcend "the sex talk," it would be good to pause for a moment and consider

---

[36] This list, and the summary before it, is only a cursory overview of the bulk of John Paul II's first chapter of *Theology of the Body*, especially 149–166.

[37] John Paul II, apostolic exhortation *Familiaris Consortio* (November 22, 1981), no. 11.

God's creative wisdom from a different angle. We need to con-sider how people, as male and female, are personally—not just sexually—complementary.

Complementarity and the Human Person

Complements are things that, when brought together, make a complete whole. Sometimes these things are parts: parts of the body, car parts, or ingredients for a loaf of bread. Alone, these parts are mere potential. They have no story of their own to tell. Sometimes, however, complements are in and of themselves whole. A forest is made of trees; each tree shares common prop-erties with the others and has distinct differences as well. This latter kind of complementarity is called *integral complementarity*.

The Genesis story of creation is a primordial lesson in integral complementarity. Time is marked by distinct periods of light and dark. The earth is carved by land and sea, with each producing its own ecosystem. Remarkably, there is no antagonism between the separated elements. Day and night do not compete for the primacy of time telling, and neither land nor sea is lord of the other. Rather, they are symbiotic. This was the way of the natural world, until the appearance of man.

The creation of man marks a significant departure in God's creative wisdom. God willed man to be a part of the visible world but also to have a unique share in His life. Man was the bridge between the visible world and the invisible world, between Heaven and Earth, between God and all of creation: he was the image and likeness of God. During his time of original solitude, Adam's endeavor to know and name all living creatures ended with an emerging understanding of the distinctive quality that made man the visible likeness of the invisible God: the ability to know and to deliberately use that knowledge; Western philosophy calls this rationality. What's important about this is that even though man has this elevated position in creation, God still saw fit to create man as integral complements. This means that the two particular ways of being a human — male and female — are vital to man's ability to inhabit both the visible and invisible world.

What we see in man's creation, then, is the union of complements upon complements. A body and a rational soul come together in Adam and then in Woman. As soon as Adam sees Woman, the full story of humanity is completed. But where is the wisdom in creating man and woman separately, when the differences are marginal compared with the rest of nature's complements? The integral complementarity of day and night, for example, is precisely in the stark contrast between the two. As with yin and yang, what is common to both is secondary to what makes them different. Comparatively, the differences between man and woman are subtle. There is so much more that man and woman have in common that it takes effort to identify what makes each unique. It seems an odd choice for God to risk redundancy when He willed His image to be revealed in man and woman. It is odd, until we consider the fact that the creation of man as male and female is told in not one but two chapters of Genesis—two *integrally complementary* chapters! It is possible that the structure, tone, and content of each version of creation, and how they complement each other, holds the key to understanding man and woman's complementarity as persons. Let's look closely at these chapters.

Genesis 1 reads like a textbook. Each day of creation is presented chronologically, making it possible to observe how the next day builds upward and outward from the preceding day, culminating in the creation of man. The descriptions of each day are also very detailed and functional. For example, the description of the third day of creation is a lesson in basic geology and botany:

> And God said, "Let the waters under the heavens be gathered together into one place, and let the dry land appear." And it was so. God called the dry land Earth, and the waters that were gathered together he called Seas. And God saw that it was good. And God said, "Let the earth put forth vegetation, plants yielding seed, and fruit trees bearing fruit in which is their seed, each according to its kind, upon the earth." And it was so. The earth brought forth vegetation, plants yielding seed according to their own kinds, and trees bearing fruit in which is their seed, each according to its kind. And God saw that it was good. And there was evening and there was morning, a third day. (vv. 9–13)

Finally, much of the language is repetitious. Every day of creation begins with "And God said" and ends with "And there was evening and there was morning, [an nth] day." Neither does a day end without acknowledging that "God saw that it was good." Other examples, of varying frequency, include "and it was so" and "be fruitful and multiply."

From this brief analysis, it appears that Genesis 1 is oriented toward a specific kind of knowledge about creation. It is scientific in nature: the technical aspects of creation are enumerated—the what and the how. The earth was separated from the heavens by a firmament; the seas were contained by land masses, and the sun and the moon governed the days, nights, and seasons.

Genesis 2, on the other hand, is oriented toward a contextual understanding of creation, specifically that of man. The account narrows its focus to the apex of the sixth day of creation, when man is made in God's image and likeness, yet it takes 541 words to impart the same truth that Genesis 1 did in 72 words. It engages almost all of our senses by replacing repetition with description:

> In the day that the LORD God made the earth and the heavens, when no plant of the field was yet in the earth and no herb of the field had yet sprung up—for the LORD God had not caused it to rain upon the earth, and there was no man to till the ground; but a mist went up from the earth and watered the whole face of the ground—then the LORD God formed man of dust from the ground, and breathed into his nostrils the breath of life; and man became a living being. (vv. 4–7)

This account draws us into the drama of creation, making the experience personal. It recounts what happened and helps us understand its value, or why God made the world as He did. The trees and the plants were good because they were pretty to look at and provided food to eat. The living creatures were made to help man know his unique dignity and vocation in the world, and Woman was created to help Adam articulate that dignity and vocation and to live it out with him.

We can summarize the integral complementarity of the two accounts of creation by their relationship to three fundamental elements of the story: *what* is happening, *how* it happens, and *why* it matters. Both accounts share the general subject of *what* God did with His creative wisdom, and both posit man at the apex of creation. What makes Genesis 1 and 2 significantly different is that the first account emphasizes *how* God's creative wisdom came about over *why* it mattered, whereas the second account does the opposite. For example, compare Genesis 1:12 and Genesis 2:9:

The earth brought forth vegetation, plants yielding seed according to their own kinds, and trees bearing fruit in which is their seed, each according to its kind.

And out of the ground the LORD God made to grow every tree that is pleasant to the sight and good for food.

Another notable example is that Genesis 1 tells us six times that God's creation is good, but Genesis 2 does not directly address it. Instead, Genesis 2 offers an explanation for the nature of God's goodness by recognizing that "it is not good that the man should be alone" and describing how the lack of goodness was remedied. Clearly, elements of *how* and *why* exist in both accounts, but the manifest difference in emphasis allows them to stand on their own as full stories. Neither account is dependent on the other for completion, nor is one better than the other. The beauty of their complementarity is that when the full measure of each is brought together with the other, another complete and unique story emerges.

The complementary accounts of creation make compelling parallels to the complementarity of Adam and Woman. Like the first account of creation, Adam appears first and spends his time in original solitude, ordering the visible things of the world. Tasked with the cultivation and care of Eden, he establishes the pattern for agrarian life: when to plant, when to harvest, and when to rest. Given every living creature as a "help," Adam orders them, too, by giving them names. It's not until God creates Woman and brings her to him that we get a definitive sense of how inclined toward orderliness Adam is. As with the other living creatures, Adam names Woman, but this time he reveals his process for choosing an appropriate name: "She shall be called Woman because she was taken out of Man." This is not a boast; sin has not yet entered the world, making man and woman competitors for dominance. It is a simple observation about the nature of Woman's creation. Assuming that his naming process was the same for the other living creatures as it was for Woman, it's reasonable to infer that Adam ordered the visible things of the world according to their biological nature.

Before Woman, Adam was functional but not fulfilled. He knew what to do and how to do it, but something was hovering around him, just out of reach. It was a sense of purpose: *why* God created him. This was the story that Woman was created to tell: "This at last is bone of my bones and flesh of my flesh." Without saying a single word or doing anything other than *existing*, Woman reveals to Adam that God willed humanity to life "in his own image." She reveals that the goodness of creation is in communion, and the goodness of communion between man and woman is both physical and rational. She is man's gateway between the visible and the invisible.

What we find in these two accounts of humanity is the same what-how-why formulation, with Adam's account skewing *what-how*-why and Woman's account more *what*-how-*why*.

This does not mean that God intended for men to be linear thinkers without emotive capabilities and that women were created to be feelers with the occasional rational insight. These tropes are the effects of sin; in later chapters, we will explore how deeply evil insinuates itself into society's understanding of sex and the human person. But we *can* imagine how man lived out integral complementarity in the time before Original Sin, because without sin, there was no strife. Adam and Woman didn't feel the need to fight about who fed the cattle and who turned over the soil. There was no debate about whose job it was to make dinner, or who was supposed to collect wood, or who was responsible for delivering the animals' young, because nothing was specifically "assigned" to one or the other. Work was done, food was consumed, joy was shared, rest was enjoyed—together. If we understand male-female complementarity in this way, as whole persons, it is easier to see why Christ broke with social convention to include women in ministry and laud their singular witnesses of faith. It makes more sense why the Church would break with societal expectations and encourage young women to consider sacrificing marriage for the religious life. And it perfectly sets the stage for John Paul II to repeatedly affirm throughout his papacy that

> the lay faithful, in fact, "are called by God so that they, led by the spirit of the Gospel, might contribute to the sanctification of the world, as from within like leaven, by fulfilling their own particular duties. Thus, especially in this way of life, resplendent in faith, hope and charity they manifest Christ to others." Thus for the lay faithful, to be present and active in the world is not only an anthropological and sociological reality, but in a specific way, a theological and ecclesiological reality as well. In fact, in their situation in the world God manifests his plan and communicates to them their particular vocation of "seeking the Kingdom of God by engaging in temporal affairs and by ordering them according to the plan of God." ... It should in fact be clear that "when women are able fully to share their gifts with the whole community, the very way in which society understands and organizes itself is improved."[38]

[38] *Christifideles Laici*, nos. 15, 40.

3

Present in a Hidden Way

Poor Eve. Would that we were able to contemplate and appreciate the richness of her incomparable human value to creation in God's image and likeness and enjoy the clear and unfettered richness of this value in our own lives! Instead, we are obliged to contemplate her role in the introduction of sin into the world, and the legacy of her choice: pain, death, confusion, and strife. The Fall of Adam and Eve devastated the human experience. The knowledge and peace that come with a clear vision of the dignity and purpose of the human person, both male and female, as Genesis shows, are the gateway to an understanding of God's own self and image; the loss of this clarity is the cradle of all future sins.

This makes God's first promise of redemption, the Protoevangelium, all the more fitting, because the victory over evil must come from the combined efforts of man and woman: "I will put enmity between you and the woman, and between your seed and her seed; he shall bruise your head, and you shall bruise his heel" (Gen. 3:15). From the very moment of the Fall, God tasks every man and woman with actively participating in his or her salvation. The battle with evil is both an individual one and a collaborative one. All are called to bruise the head of the serpent.

All are called to have enmity for the serpent and to preserve and transmit that enmity from one generation to the next. This is the essence of the Old Covenant, recorded in the Old Testament Scriptures—that God's people would do what our first parents could not: put God first in all things and at all times.

Ultimately, the promise of redemption and the defeat of evil is brought to fruition by the Incarnation of Jesus Christ through the Blessed Virgin Mary, but that does not mean that salvation history prior to the advent of Christ was devoid of any progress toward redemption. In fact, the history of God's Chosen People that is preserved in the Old Testament Scriptures is nothing less than a preparation for humanity to reencounter the fullness of divine truth. The Old Testament Scriptures

> reveal to all men the knowledge of God and of man and the ways in which God, just and merciful, deals with men.... [They] give expression to a lively sense of God, contain a store of sublime teachings about God, sound wisdom about human life, and a wonderful treasury of prayers, and in them the mystery of our salvation is present in a hidden way. God ... wisely arranged that the New Testament be hidden in the Old and the Old be made manifest in the New. For, though Christ established the new covenant in His blood ... the books of the Old Testament with all their parts, caught up into the proclamation of the Gospel, acquire and show forth their full meaning in the New Testament ... and in turn shed light on it and explain it.[39]

---

[39] Second Vatican Council, Dogmatic Constitution on Divine Revelation *Dei Verbum* (November 18, 1965), nos. 15–16.

Memorable Women of the Old Testament

"The mystery of our salvation is present in a hidden way." Tied up in this mystery is the mystery of the feminine genius, which John Paul II lauded in myriad ways and on multiple occasions. The Old Testament Scriptures offer fascinating insights into God's gradual restoration of womanhood through the cooperation of a number of memorable women. In fact, some of the more crucial moments in Israel's history were decided in their favor because of the cooperative intervention of God and a woman. The precise nature of this cooperation is both wholly human and distinctly feminine; the preservation of their stories in Scripture mark these women as those who lead us closer to the full meaning of womanhood. Let's focus on a few of the most memorable: Hannah, Deborah and Jael, Ruth, Esther, Judith, and Susanna.

Hannah (1 Samuel 1–2)

We meet Hannah at a particularly trying time of her life. Married and unable to bear children, she is shamed and ridiculed for her barrenness. Her husband's other wife, Peninnah, often likes to "provoke her sorely, to irritate her, because the LORD had closed her womb" (1:6). Hannah feels cursed by God and mourns her predicament deeply. After years of this, during a pilgrimage to the temple at Shiloh, Peninnah's harassment becomes too much for Hannah. Weeping and refusing to eat, she goes to the temple to pray before the Lord. Pouring out her heart and soul, she makes a vow: "O LORD of hosts, if thou wilt indeed look on the affliction of thy maidservant, and remember me, and not forget thy maidservant, but wilt give to thy maidservant a son, then I will give him to the LORD all the days of his life, and no razor shall touch his head" (1:11). When she finishes praying, Hannah is no longer sad. Soon afterward, Hannah and her husband conceive

Samuel. When the child is old enough to be weaned, Hannah fulfills her vow and takes Samuel to the temple, delivering him to the temple priest, Eli. Samuel goes on to become a great prophet and the last judge of Israel, ushering in the centralization of power among the tribes under a monarchy.

Deborah and Jael (Judges 4–5)

Deborah is a woman of extraordinary influence. In the first place, she is a prophetess—one "supernaturally enlightened"[40] to interpret and announce God's will for Israel, teach the Old Law, and guide the people away from iniquity in preparation for the coming Messiah. On top of this, she has the distinction of being a judge: a deliverer of the Chosen People from God's enemies. As a judge, she delivers the tribes of Israel from decades of Canaanite oppression, directing her general, Barak, on the strategy for victory. Deborah's influence is so powerful that Barak refuses to carry out God's will unless she is present, as if she is a visible sign—much like the ark—of divine favor. This dependency on the woman who "arose as a mother in Israel" (5:7) leads Deborah to prophesy that victory over Israel's enemy will be at the hands of a woman.

That woman turns out to be Jael, the wife of Heber the Kenite, a descendant of Moses' father-in-law, Jethro. The Canaanite general, Sisera, stumbles into her tent while fleeing from his army's crushing defeat. Her allegiances are unknown. At first, it appears that she is a Canaanite sympathizer; she feeds and shelters Sisera, offering him rest. Only after she drives a tent spike through his temple and delivers the body into the hands of Barak

---

[40] J. M. Calès, "Prophecy, Prophet, and Prophetess," *Catholic Encyclopedia* (New York: Robert Appleton, 1911), http://www.newadvent.org/cathen/12477a.htm.

do we discover that Jael is an agent of God. She is remembered as the "most blessed of women" because "she crushed his head" (5:24, 26).

Ruth (Book of Ruth)

Ruth is a Moabite, of a people forbidden to "enter the assembly of the LORD for ever," according to Mosaic law (Deut. 23:3). Despite her nationality, she finds herself married to the younger son of a Jewish family who emigrates to Moab after famine strikes Judea. Ten years of an ordinary life with her husband, her mother-in-law, Naomi, and her brother-in-law and his Moabite wife, Orpha, pass before both of Naomi's sons die. Naomi, hearing that Judea has food again, decides to return to the land of her people. Knowing the hardship that awaits her daughters-in-law, as both Moabites and widows, if they traveled with her, she tells them to return to their mothers' houses, where they will be cared for and be able to find new husbands. Orpha eventually accepts Naomi's wisdom and returns home. Ruth, on the other hand, decides to leave the comfort of her native home, her people, and the faith of the Moabites to stay with Naomi and journey toward a new home, with a new people and a new religion. Not even the possibility of death will deter her from doing this (1:17). Because of her decision, Ruth brings joy and peace back into Naomi's life. And unknown to her, Ruth's choice leads her to become the great-grandmother of King David and to foreshadow the inclusion of Gentiles in Christ's salfivic mission.

Esther (Book of Esther)

In Persia, a beautiful young Hebrew woman named Hadassah finds herself forced into bondage as a potential member of the harem of King Xerxes. Advised by her uncle to keep her Jewish heritage a secret, she goes by the Persian name Esther. When Xerxes decides to choose a new queen from among the women of the harem, Esther rivets his attention: "The king loved Esther more than all the women, and she found grace and favor in his sight more than all the virgins, so that he set the royal crown on her head and made her queen" (2:17). When Esther's uncle disrupts a plot to assassinate the king and incurs the wrath of the king's enemy against all Jews, he begs Esther to intercede on behalf of her people. Despite fearing the potential death sentence of approaching the king without first being summoned by him, Esther chooses to become an instrument of deliverance for her people. After fasting and praying for three days and nights, she approaches the king. She exposes the king's true enemies and earns for her people a chance to defend themselves against an impending attack. After her people's victory, Esther and her uncle establish the feast of Purim as a yearly commemoration of "the days on which the Jews got relief from their enemies, and as the month that had been turned for them from sorrow into gladness and from mourning into a holiday" (9:22).

Judith (Book of Judith)

Judith is a wealthy, respected widow living a quiet life of fasting and prayer in the Judean mountain town of Bethulia when the people of Israel receive the news that the Assyrian king and his general, Holofernes, are laying waste to every nation that refuses to serve the king, and that Holofernes is at Judea's doorstep. Known as a beauty, Judith is also considered "prudent of heart, discerning in judgment, and quite virtuous.... No one spoke ill of her, for she feared God with great devotion" (8:7–8). When her people begin to give in to fear of Holofernes and his terrible army and, losing faith in God, plan to surrender to the enemy,

Judith employs her virtuous and prudent temperament to rouse her kinsmen from sin:

> Who are you, that have put God to the test this day, and are setting yourselves up in the place of God among the sons of men? You are putting the Lord Almighty to the test—but you will never know anything! You cannot plumb the depths of the human heart, nor find out what a man is thinking; how do you expect to search out God, who made all these things, and find out his mind or comprehend his thought?... Do not try to bind the purposes of the Lord our God; for God is not like man, to be threatened, nor like a human being, to be won over by pleading. Therefore, while we wait for his deliverance, let us call upon him to help us, and he will hear our voice, if it pleases him.... In spite of everything let us give thanks to the Lord our God, who is putting us to the test as he did our forefathers.... The Lord scourges those who draw near to him, in order to admonish them. (8:12–14, 16–17, 25, 27)

These are not empty words; Judith also has a plan. After prostrating herself in prayer and asking God to reveal His glory and might through the work of her hands, Judith infiltrates Holofernes's camp by pretending to be a defector. With her beauty and her promise to hand over vital information that the general can use to crush the Hebrews, she charms everyone in the enemy camp. She is allowed to eat her own food, avoiding anything unclean according to the law, and is given permission to wander outside the encampment to pray. Judith maintains this routine for days, lulling Holofernes and the soldiers into trusting her. It is not long before Holofernes desires to possess Judith. Inviting her into his tent, he asks Judith to drink with him. She accepts, for the first time, and Holofernes is so pleased at this development that he gets drunk. Alone together, with the general in a stupor, Judith decapitates Holofernes with his own sword. Concealing the head in a bag, she brings it back to her people with instructions to display the head on the parapet wall and prepare to march into battle. Without their leader, the Assyrian army attempts to flee but instead is decimated by the Hebrews.

Susanna (Daniel 13)

Susanna is beautiful, well versed in Mosaic law, and married to a wealthy and influential elder. Two other elders who frequently work with Susanna's husband become infatuated with Susanna, spying on her during her daily walks through her husband's garden. Upon discovering each other's desire for the same woman, they conspire to force themselves on Susanna. They find an opportunity one day when she decides to bathe alone in the garden pool. Approaching Susanna, the wicked elders leave her with an impossible decision to make: "Give your consent, and lie with us. If you refuse, we will testify against you that a young man was with you" (vv. 20–21). Knowing that either choice will lead to a death sentence, Susanna decides to retain her integrity before God and refuses the elders' advances. She is brought before the elders for judgment; the wicked elders' testimony and their social status ensure a judgment of death for Susanna. Susanna never addresses the elders and others who gathered for her judgment. Her defense is made only to God: "O eternal God, who discern what is secret, who are aware of all things before they come to be, you know that these men have borne false witness against me. And now I am to die! Yet I have done none of the things that they have wickedly invented against me!" (see vv. 42–43).

God hears her and sends the young prophet Daniel to prove her innocence in the eyes of men. He does; and the wicked elders are put to death, Susanna's blamelessness is celebrated, and "all the assembly shouted loudly and blessed God" (v. 60).

Redemptive Agency of the Old Covenant Woman

These women represent the spectrum of a stereotypically feminine experience. They are socioeconomically diverse. Some are married, happily or not; two are widows. Half of them enjoy a significant amount of social influence; the others have limited freedom within the established patriarchy. What unites these women is their singular ability to further God's self-revelation to the world, *in their own right*. None of these women speaks or acts for the beneficial advancement of a man. Their stories are preserved so that we remember *them*, not what kind of children they bore. Hannah is a perfect example. She is unique among the mothers of the great Old Testament figures because, while brief, her story enables us to get to know her on a deeply personal level. We witness how she acts under stress, and the words she chooses to express her joys and sorrows. No other mother is given the same amount of space to come alive in our minds. Saul's, David's, and Solomon's mothers are barely mentioned, if they are mentioned at all. We can make educated guesses about Sarah and Leah, but nothing more.

Together, this group of women reveals an interesting pattern of thought and agency that is distinctly different from that of their male counterparts. Notably, they do so despite utilizing the same graces and human abilities as men do. These women pray, just like men. They advise and admonish, just like men. They believe in the same God and live by the same law. The distinction—and its importance — is not what these women say and do but how they say and do it. This distinctiveness manifests itself in their personal integrity and in their relationship with God.

Personal Integrity

Starting with Abram, God calls His people to "walk before me, and be blameless" (Gen. 17:1). The people of Israel heed His call, for a while, until their hearts grow weak. The Old Testament relates the cyclical ebb and flow of Israel's adherence to God's call: covenantal peace broken by rebellion and reconciled after God's punishment and the people's repentance. Men such as Jacob, Moses, Job, David, and Solomon represent humanity's struggle to walk blamelessly before God, giving witness to the reality of our broken nature and the need to rely on God's infinite mercy. Interestingly, the women of the Old Testament do not share in this representation. They — down to a woman — appear to inhabit the extremes: either blameless or full of iniquity.

Hannah, Deborah, Jael, Ruth, Esther, Judith, and Susanna are, by the intentions and standards of the Old Testament,[41] blameless. The absolute personal integrity of each woman is woven into every narrative. Deborah and Jael, about whom we know the least, communicate this integrity implicitly; the quality of their character is proven by what God brings about by their hands.

---

[41] When it comes to reconciling the righteousness of Old Testament figures with their sinful actions (lying and murder are the most common), the Church recognizes and affirms the inherent evil of such actions; God does not approve of the evil actions, only of the purity of faith on display. Christ, as sole mediator and perfect sacrifice, puts an end to any allowance for sinful actions done in righteousness.

Hannah also communicates her integrity through action — or rather, inaction. She never retaliates against or returns insults to her husband's other wife for her cruelty. The others are openly lauded for their blamelessness. Ruth is "a woman of worth" (Ruth 3:11) because she remains loyal to Naomi, and to the Hebrew faith, despite the danger this poses. Susanna's supposed adultery was shameful to her servants because it was out of character for "one who feared the Lord" (Dan. 13:2). Esther is "perfect in faith"[42] because she refused to allow her circumstances to tempt her away from God: "I hate the splendor of the wicked.... I abhor the sign of my proud position.... Your servant has had no joy since the day that I was brought here until now, except in you, O Lord God of Abraham" (Est. 14:15–16, 18). And Judith is "the exaltation of Jerusalem" because "from the beginning of your life all the people have recognized your understanding, for your heart's disposition is right" (Jth. 15:9; 8:29).

The absolute nature of their personal integrity is plain. These women don't waver in their faith or doubt their abilities. Neither do they ever compromise their covenantal relationship with God by sinning. Moreover, their stories imply that Hannah, Deborah, Jael, Ruth, Esther, Judith, and Susanna's integrity has a perpetual quality to it: they are always, and in every circumstance, blameless. Ruth is a fitting example. As a Moabite, she is a stranger and enemy to the Hebrew faith. But as a person, Ruth naturally embodies the Ten Commandments. She rejects the Moabite gods for the one God and honors her mother-in-law. She is honest and chaste with Boaz, neither stealing from him nor seducing him as a means to care for Naomi. What's more, Ruth appears to give no thought to what she does or consider whether she should act

---

[42] Clement of Rome, *Letter to the Corinthians: First Epistle*, chap. 55.

differently; she simply acts as she does. It's reflexive — as natural as breathing. This is true for all of these women. The outpouring of their integrity into actions that directly influence the salvation of God's people is not turned on and off, as with David and Solomon: it flows like a river. As Old Testament figures, these women are unique in this regard because, as their stories indicate, their relationships with God are unique.

Relationship with God

God clearly and repeatedly insists on His primacy of place in the lives of His people. This prescription is the first of the Ten Commandments: "I am the LORD your God.... You shall have no other gods before me" (Exod. 20:2–3). This is the first prescription Moses handed down to the Israelites; we know it by rote. Not as well known is that Moses provided Israel with two versions of the First Commandment. The first, more familiar, version is negative; we learn what we should not do. The second version is positive: "You shall love the LORD your God with all your heart, and with all your soul, and with all your might" (Deut. 6:5). Both versions communicate the same essential message, that God comes first, but the underlying context of each version affects our understanding of God and our subsequent response of faith.

Call it a shift of perspective. The first version communicates supremacy, loyalty, obedience, and — God freely admits — a just jealousy (Exod. 20:5; Deut. 5:9). It instills a sense of hierarchy but also a sense of security and belonging: if God is *my* God, that means I am *His*. And as long as I remain His, He remains with me. As a result, the proper response of faith is to submit our minds and wills to God and His law. This is the nature of the covenantal relationship we see established between God and Abraham, Isaac, and Jacob: a type of passive adherence to God's magnanimity. On the other hand, the second version is an explicit call to radical self-gift: to pour out our whole selves to God and create a relationship of communion with Him. It communicates intimacy, fidelity, and totality. It is *active*. And rather than contradicting the covenantal relationship communicated in the first version, the second version assumes that obedience of faith to God and His law naturally emanates from those who love Him with all their hearts, souls, and might.

The relationships that Hannah, Deborah, Jael, Ruth, Esther, Judith, and Susanna have with God are of the latter kind. Their blamelessness strongly suggests it: it's significant that these women never fall into idol worship, or succumb to bodily temptations of any magnitude, or compromise the law to allow for Israel's hardened heart. Their prayers, however, confirm that these women are each in a relationship of communion with God. Within the six prayers that are preserved, each woman acknowledges her lowly position—Hannah the "maidservant," Judith the "widow," Susanna the falsely accused, and Esther the "orphan"—yet speaks to God, and of God, in ways that indicate a stronger bond than the kind between master and servant. First, these women communicate a superabundance of trust in God. Hannah, Judith, Susanna, and Esther are in dire situations that don't seem to have feasible remedies. Hannah is a few thousand years away from Natural Procreative (NaPro) Technology, and Susanna's word means nothing to the tribunal against respected tribal elders, especially without evidence. Both Judith and Esther face powerful, dangerous men, with the impending genocide of the Hebrew people lurking in each man's shadow. But, as if by instinct, the first thing each woman does is turn to God. Like drops into a reservoir, they pour out themselves and their plight before God; they seek His intervention and offer themselves as cooperators. Hannah, for example, prays for a son, vowing to give the child back to the "LORD of hosts" if he deigns to answer her (1 Sam. 1:11). After receiving that son, she enfolds herself within all that God has done for His faithful ones:

> There is none holy like the LORD, there is none besides you; there is no rock like our God. Talk no more so very proudly, let not arrogance come from your mouth; for the LORD is a God of knowledge, and by him actions are weighed. The bows of the mighty are broken, but the feeble gird on strength. Those who were full have hired themselves out for bread, but those who were hungry have ceased to hunger. The barren has borne seven, but she who has many children is forlorn. The LORD kills and brings to life; he brings down to Sheol and raises up. The LORD makes poor and makes rich; he brings low, he also exalts. He raises up the poor from the dust; he lifts the needy from the ash heap, to make them sit with princes and inherit a seat of honor. For the pillars of the earth are the LORD's, and on them he has set the world. (see 1 Sam 2:2–8)

All four women offer prayers of petition, rooting themselves in God and His agency. Once their petitions are made, every woman does something remarkable: she leaves it all with God—the fear, the sadness, and the anger—and moves forward with her life. After Hannah prays and speaks to the priest Eli, she "went her way and ate, and her countenance was no longer sad" (1 Sam. 1:18). After three days of fasting and prayer, Esther "took off the garments in which she had worshiped, and arrayed herself in splendid attire" (Esther 15:1). Susanna resigns herself to whatever God allows to happen to her, and Judith jumps into action:

> She rose from where she lay prostrate and called her maid and went down into the house where she lived on sabbaths and on her feast days; and she removed the sackcloth which she had been wearing, and took off her widow's garments, and bathed her body with water, and anointed herself with precious ointment, and combed her hair and put on a tiara, and arrayed herself in her gayest apparel. (Jth. 10:2–3)

It takes an incredible amount of trust in someone to be able to leave your worries with that person and come away nearly unburdened—an unequivocal confidence in his ability to make your situation better. That level of trust comes only with deep, personal intimacy: a vulnerability and openness between two people in which each knows the other well and the relationship is comfortable. It is the intimacy of friendship. Hannah, Judith, Susanna, and Esther feel comfortable with God and trust Him as a close friend.

It is also apparent that these women are just as worried, if not more so, about how their plight affects God as about how it affects them. Esther laments Israel's bondage under Persia, but she admits the justice of it as punishment for Israel's idol worship. What horrifies her and spurs her to action is what the Persians intend to do to God:

> And now they are not satisfied that we are in bitter slavery, but they have covenanted with their idols to abolish what your mouth has ordained and to destroy your inheritance, to stop the mouths of those who praise you

and to quench your altar and the glory of your house, to open the mouths of the nations for the praise of vain idols, and to magnify for ever a mortal king. (see Est. 14:8–10)

Judith is likewise provoked by the injustices Holofernes and his army commit against God:

They glory in the strength of their foot soldiers; they trust in shield and spear, in bow and sling, and know not that you are the Lord who crushes wars; the Lord is your name. Break their strength by your might, and bring down their power in your anger; for they intend to defile your sanctuary and to pollute the tabernacle where your glorious name rests, and to cast down the horn of your altar with the sword. Behold their pride, and send your wrath upon their heads.... Make my deceitful words to be their wound and stripe, for they have planned cruel things against your covenant, and against your consecrated house, and against the top of Zion, and against the house possessed by your children. (see Jth. 9:7–9, 13)

Susanna prefers death at the hands of men over contradicting the "eternal God, who discerns what is secret, who is aware of all things before they come to be" (see Dan. 13:42), and Hannah's desire for a child is the desire to receive from God so that she can give right back to Him.

No prayers from Deborah, Jael, and Ruth are preserved, but their lives communicate the same essential message. As both prophetess and judge, Deborah's intimacy with God is almost unrivaled. God entrusts His will and His people to her, and, in turn, Deborah speaks and acts with unconditional faith in the absolute truth of what God communicates to her. She never hesitates or questions her ability to carry out God's will. Ruth's relationship with Naomi and the choices she makes for the good of that relationship are a material image of the spiritual friendship with God communicated by Hannah, Judith, Susanna, and Esther. And Jael, as prophesied, is Israel's saving agent under God's providence.

The close friendship these women have with God and their ability continually to walk blamelessly before Him presume one thing: that Hannah, Deborah, Jael, Ruth, Esther, Judith, and Susanna have a penetrating knowledge of God. Deborah is the only prophetess in the group, yet all of the women appear to understand God's precise will in their given circumstances and know how to respond, as if the knowledge is infused into their souls. Judith has her plan ready when she prepares her people and petitions God, as does Esther. Hannah understands that if God gives her a son, then he is meant for more than a normal life. Each of them is, in a sense, of one mind and one heart with God. Though it's not framed this way in their stories, what we witness in these women is the operative harmony between the virtues of knowledge, understanding, wisdom, and counsel — gifts of the Holy Spirit. They are living examples of a process that St. Thomas Aquinas explained:

> But faith, first and principally, is about the First Truth, secondarily, about certain considerations concerning creatures, and furthermore extends to the direction of human actions, in so far as it works through charity.... Accordingly ... two things are requisite on our part: first that they be penetrated or grasped by the intellect, and this belongs to the gift of understanding. Secondly, it is necessary that man should judge these things aright, that

he should esteem that he ought to adhere to these things, and to withdraw from their opposites: and this judgment with regard to Divine things belongs to the gift of wisdom, but with regard to created things, belongs to the gift of knowledge, and as to its application to individual actions, belongs to the gift of counsel.[43]

The distinctive qualities that these women share—the gifts of faith, a close relationship with God, and perpetual blameless-ness—are not found in any other person in the Old Testament, at least not in the way and to the degree displayed by Hannah, Deborah, Jael, Ruth, Esther, Judith, and Susanna. These seven women are guideposts throughout early salvation history, laying out the trajectory of womanhood in the divine plan. God hides the mystery of womanhood in plain sight so that, when the time comes, the revelation of the fullness of womanhood can both inform and be informed by the witness of these women.

---

[43] *Summa Theologica*, II-II, q. 8, art. 6.

4

Theotokos

Long after the lives of Hannah, Deborah, Jael, Ruth, Esther, Judith, and Susanna fade from living memory, the Protoevange‑ lium—ancient even in their day—comes to fulfillment in the unassuming village of Nazareth. A girl is born; her parents name her Mary. She grows and is betrothed to Joseph, a carpenter. Before they are married, an angel of God announces to Mary that she has been chosen to be the mother of the Messiah, the one who will bruise the head of the serpent:

> Hail, full of grace, the Lord is with you!... Do not be afraid, Mary, for you have found favor with God. And behold, you will conceive in your womb and bear a son, and you shall call his name Jesus. He will be great, and will be called the Son of the Most High; and the Lord God will give to him the throne of his father David, and he will reign over the house of Jacob for ever; and of his kingdom there will be no end. (Luke 1:28, 30–33)

Mary replies, "Behold, I am the handmaid of the Lord; let it be to me according to your word (Luke 1:38). With these words, she becomes the Theotokos, the Mother of God, and the first to give witness to the gospel message: *Deus fit homo ut homo fieret*

Deus—God deigned to partake of our human nature so we may become partakers of His divine nature.[44]

Theotokos is Mary's most ancient title, and its strict translation is "God bearer." Rich with literal and symbolic meaning, the Greek word became a definitive addition to the Church's doctrinal vocabulary in A.D. 431 at the Council of Ephesus; it perfectly preserves and professes the truth about Jesus' divine and human natures. The title also communicates profound truths about who Mary is. As the "model of the Church in the matter of faith, charity, and perfect union with Christ,"[45] Mary is a person with universal significance. She guides everyone in the ways of discipleship: of bearing God through faith and deeds, bringing ourselves and the world into a closer relationship with Jesus. At the same time, the Mother of God intercedes for her adopted children (John 19:26–27), bringing all of their needs "within the radius of Christ's messianic mission and salvific power … place[ing] herself between her Son and mankind in the reality of their wants, needs, and sufferings."[46] The Church also affirms that Mary embodies the "fullness of the perfection of what is characteristic of [a] woman."[47] Women on both sides of the Incarnation coalesce around her; Hannah, Deborah, Jael, Ruth, Esther, Judith, and Susanna point to Mary, and the women who

[44] The Latin phrase, literally "God became man so that man might become God," is a summation of how the Church Fathers communicate Christ's salvific mission, from the Incarnation to His death and Resurrection; it is consistent with Jesus' admissions (see John 6:46; 14:6; Rom. 8:15). The Fathers include, but aren't limited to, St. Irenaeus of Lyons, St. Clement of Alexandria, St. Hilary of Poitiers, St. Gregory of Nyssa, and St. Augustine.

[45] *Redemptoris Mater*, nos. 5–6.

[46] Ibid., no. 21.

[47] *Mulieris Dignitatem*, no. 5.

come after Mary draw inspiration and support from her. Here, as with her universal significance, Mary's title of Theotokos penetrates to the deepest truths about the agency of womanhood in the divine plan.

First and foremost, the Theotokos is Eve's antithesis.[48] She bears God into the world rather than bringing in all that is diametrically opposed to Him: sin and death. Mary ushers in the New Covenant; in her, we "return to that 'beginning' in which one finds the 'woman' as she was intended to be in *creation*, and therefore in the eternal mind of God: in the bosom of the Most Holy Trinity."[49] But Mary does not wipe the slate clean. She does not invalidate who Eve was *supposed* to be or make the lives of the righteous Old Testament women — known and unknown — a wasted effort. What Mary does, especially as the Theotokos, is give us a new lens to peer through, in order to make just observations about womanhood.

Looking back at the Old Testament seven — Hannah, Deborah, Jael, Ruth, Esther, Judith, and Susanna — we see that the Theotokos both confirms and perfects their prophetic feminine agency. These women of the Old Testament walk blamelessly before God; Mary is blameless from conception. Echoes of Hannah's prayers are in Mary's song of praise,[50] and Elizabeth's greeting to

---

[48] Irenaeus, *Against Heresies*, trans. Alexander Roberts and William Rambaut, bk. 3, chap. 22, in *Ante-Nicene Fathers*, vol. 1, *The Apostolic Fathers with Justin Martyr and Irenaeus*, ed. Alexander Roberts, James Donaldson, and A. Cleveland Coxe (Buffalo, NY: Christian Literature Publishing, 1885), 455.

[49] *Mulieris Dignitatem*, no. 11.

[50] See Luke 1:46–55; "1 Kings 1," in *A Catholic Commentary on Holy Scripture*, ed. Dom Bernard Orchard (New York: Thomas Nelson and Sons, 1953), 308.

The Supreme Vocation of Women

Mary — "blessed are you among women" — is the same one given to Judith and Jael. Comparisons like these abound, but the most striking one is the radical intimacy with which these women bear God in the world. God flows through them in ways unseen in any other person who is not God Himself. Mary's God-bearing is both perfectly spiritual and unabashedly literal. Her soul unites with God, and God enters the world through her, taking His human nature from hers. The relationship between God and the Old Testament seven prefigures the Theotokos with incredible exactness. Consider the most famous of the seven: Deborah, Esther, and Judith. Their God-bearing calls upon the totality of their person, soul and body, to bring forth the full force of God's will. There is no intermediary object between them, God, and what God wishes to communicate in the world: no staff, no rock, no parted waters, no plagues, no tablets. These women *are* the intermediary through which God directs others to Himself.

Womanhood, viewed through the lens of the Theotokos, takes on a sublime visage. It is an image that looks and sounds a lot like how John Paul II ultimately described women: as sentinels, standing at the sacred intersection where God and man meet. Eve completes the image of God in man; the Old Testament seven make good on their own prophetic words; the Word passes through Mary to become flesh and dwell among us. The reality of the Theotokos — the reality of what womanhood is and always has been in the divine plan — leaves no doubt about the vital agency that womanhood has in the divine purpose of the human experience.

5

"Guardians of the Gospel Message"

Today, Christ's messianic message is as familiar to us as our own reflection:

> And when the envious crafty foe
> Had marred thy noblest work below,
> Thou didst our ruined state repair
> By deigning flesh thyself to wear.
> Once of a virgin born to save,
> And now new born from death's dark grave,
> O Christ, thou bidd'st us rise with thee,
> From death to immortality.[51]

But this is not what Israel was expecting from the Messiah. God's people expected the Messiah to be a warrior-king (Num. 24:17; Ps. 45); a judge from the line of David whose throne will last forever (Isa. 11:1–6; 2 Sam. 7:11–16) and will bring peace to the world (Isa. 9:6–7). They did not expect the Messiah to be the Word made flesh, whose humanity could speak and act with divine authority;

---

[51] Stanzas 3–4 of "O Thou, the Heavens' Eternal King," in *The Hymns of the Breviary and Missal*, ed. Rev. Matthew Britt, O.S.B. (New York: Benziger Brothers, 1922), 147–148.

who came to destroy the true, eternal enemies of God—sin and death. They did not expect the poor carpenter Jesus of Nazareth.

Memorable Women of the New Testament

Despite whatever preconceived notions they had, the women who appear in the Gospels have exceptional responses to the Messiah when He arrives. A few of these women appear in multiple Gospel accounts: the hemorrhaging woman, the foreign woman, the woman who anoints Jesus in Bethany, and Mary Magdalene.

The Woman with the Hemorrhage

Sts. Matthew, Mark, and Luke recount the incident of a desperately sick woman reaching out to Jesus for healing: "And behold, a woman who had suffered from a hemorrhage for twelve years came up behind him and touched the fringe of his garment; for she said to herself, 'If I only touch his garment, I shall be made well.' Jesus turned, and seeing her he said, 'Take heart, daughter; your faith has made you well.' And instantly the woman was made well" (Matt. 9:20–22).

The Foreign Woman

Sts. Matthew and Mark preserve the story of a foreign woman—an enemy of Israel—who dares to seek Jesus' help for her possessed daughter:

> And behold, a Canaanite woman from that region came out and cried, "Have mercy on me, O Lord, Son of David; my daughter is severely possessed by a demon." But he did not answer her a word. And his disciples came and begged him, saying, "Send her away, for she is crying after us." He answered, "I was sent only to the lost sheep of the house

of Israel." But she came and knelt before him, saying, "Lord, help me." And he answered, "It is not fair to take the children's bread and throw it to the dogs." She said, "Yes, Lord, yet even the dogs eat the crumbs that fall from their master's table." Then Jesus answered her, "O woman, great is your faith! Be it done for you as you desire." And her daughter was healed instantly. (Matt. 15:22–28)

The Woman Who Anoints Jesus

All four Gospel writers share the account of a woman who anoints Jesus shortly before His Passion and death. Sts. Matthew, Mark, and John identify the woman as Mary,[52] the sister of Martha and Lazarus:

Now when Jesus was at Bethany in the house of Simon the leper, a woman came up to him with an alabaster jar of very expensive ointment, and she poured it on his head, as he sat at table. But when the disciples saw it, they were indignant, saying, "Why this waste? For this ointment might have been sold for a large sum, and given to the poor." But Jesus, aware of this, said to them, "Why do you trouble the woman? For she has done a beautiful thing to me. For you always have the poor with you, but you will not always have me. In pouring this ointment on my body she has done it to prepare me for burial. Truly, I say to you, wherever this gospel is preached in the whole world, what she has done will be told in memory of her." (Matt. 26:6–13)

[52] Scholars are uncertain whether St. Luke also speaks of Mary in his account or is thinking of a separate occasion with a different woman. See Orchard, *Catholic Commentary*, 927, 950.

The Supreme Vocation of Women

Mary Magdalene

All four Gospel accounts agree that Mary Magdalene is the first person to see Jesus resurrected and the one commissioned by Christ and His angels to give witness to the fact before the apostles:

> Mary Magdalene and the other Mary went to see the sepulchre. And behold, there was a great earthquake; for an angel of the Lord descended from heaven and came and rolled back the stone, and sat upon it.... The angel said to the women, "Do not be afraid; for I know that you seek Jesus who was crucified. He is not here; for he has risen, as he said. Come, see the place where he lay. Then go quickly and tell his disciples that he has risen from the dead, and behold, he is going before you to Galilee; there you will see him. Lo, I have told you." (Matt. 28:1–2, 5–7)

These women appear to be nothing like the righteous women of the Old Testament. They are not wealthy. They do not enjoy a high social status. There is no indication that they have reputations for being righteous pillars of the community; no one seeks their counsel or aid. They certainly aren't thwarting national dangers or decapitating generals. These women are (mostly) nameless and faceless—like the millions of women who pass through salvation history without mention. They are, in a word, ordinary. In addition, the everywoman quality is burdened by intense suffering and stigma. Mary Magdalene was believed, for centuries, to be a harlot—a reminder of the terrible condemnation of Old Testament prophets. One woman is plagued by sickness and pain that has no known cure. Another suffers the double torment of watching helplessly as a child suffers from an incurable affliction. All are judged and ridiculed and held back by those around them—not even Jesus' closest disciples can muster sympathy for the women. Instead of embodying the human ideal, according to Mosaic law, these women form a chimera of biblical society's worst fears about the human condition.

Yet Jesus makes a big deal out of these lowly women and others like them. He is impressed by them and what they do. He praises their faith and the actions that flow from it; He holds them high as exemplary witnesses to the gospel. Jesus offers the example of the poor widow who "put in everything she had" as a model of charity and generosity (Mark 12:44). Mary chose "the good portion" by sitting at Jesus' feet and later anointing him with precious oil (Luke 10:42; John 12:3). Martha, despite her tendency to worry about worldly matters, shows piercing insightfulness when faced with divine truths, as do the foreign women—the Canaanite, and the Samaritan at the well. At her brother's death, Martha does not let her grief blind her to the divine reality before her: "Lord, if you had been here, my brother would not have died. And even now I know that whatever you ask from God, God will give you.... I believe that you are the Christ, the Son of God, he who is coming into the world" (John 11:21–22, 27). And the ease with which the Samaritan woman accepts Jesus' teachings is sharply contrasted with the confusion of His own disciples when Jesus, after speaking with the woman, refuses the disciples' food, saying, "I have food to eat of which you do not know" (John 4:32).

Agency of the Gospel Women

In a brief section of *Mulieris Dignitatem* (no. 15), John Paul II contemplates the significance of these ordinary women whom

Jesus holds in high regard. The pope takes note of how they, *specifically as women,* embrace and respond to Christ's good news. Two things, intrinsically linked, stand out in these women. First is the ease with which Jesus and the women in the Gospel are able to communicate divine matters to each other. John Paul II muses:

> Christ speaks to women about the things of God, and they understand them; there is a true resonance of mind and heart, a response of faith. Jesus expresses appreciation and admiration for this distinctly "feminine" response, as in the case of the Canaanite woman. Sometimes he presents this lively faith, filled with love, as an example. *He teaches, therefore, taking as his starting-point this feminine response of mind and heart.*

The second thing that stands out in these women is the audacity of feminine faith. John Paul II mentions women such as Pilate's wife and the ones who walked the *Via Dolorosa,* who dare to protest the injustices prepared for Jesus when others are cowed into silence by the whims of the mob. He honors Martha and Mary, and St. Luke's anointing woman, who appear to embody the maxim "Practice what you preach." Two examples, in particular, resonate: the Samaritan woman at the well and the women who are present at the Crucifixion.

The Samaritan woman at the well speaks with Jesus about "the most profound mysteries of God" and, within two days, brings numerous Samaritans to belief through her testimony. John Paul II makes passing reference to the "unprecedented" nature of this circumstance; it takes a few moments for the gravity of the situation to take hold of the imagination. We have this woman—already the wrong sex for a position of teaching authority—whose difficult marital situation likely puts her in a lower social standing than other women. Then she runs into town, telling her friends and neighbors that she may have met the Messiah. To everyone who will listen to her she relates what this Jew at the well said to her in regard to divine things and her own life. *And all who hear her believe her!* The Samaritan citizens receive her testimony as if it were delivered with authority; she is as trustworthy as any scribe in handing on the sacred things of God.

The women who stand by the Cross of Jesus, John Paul II notes, far outnumber Christ's male disciples: Jesus' mother, Mary the wife of Clopas, Mary Magdalene, and a large group of women who followed Jesus throughout his ministerial wanderings. In contrast, only the beloved disciple, John, remains to watch His Lord die. John Paul II's assessment of this disparity is blunt: "As we see, in this most arduous test of faith and fidelity the women proved stronger than the Apostles. In this moment of danger, those who love much succeed in overcoming their fear."

It turns out that the women in the Gospels have a lot in common with the righteous Old Testament women—where it matters to God. The same unique intimacy is there, along with the incredible risks that come with acting on pure faith. In addition, the Gospel women and their Old Testament predecessors share another set of inclinations: protection, illumination, and relation.

Protection

People protect what is meaningful to them. What the Gospel women and their Old Testament predecessors find meaningful is the integrity of the human person. Specifically, they are profoundly empathetic to suffering and injustice; preserving the temporal, mental, and spiritual well-being of others is a top priority.

The Old Testament women have an explicit concern for the temporal welfare of others that is guided by the implicit desire for these others to remain within the safe bounds of God's ordinance. Despite the less-than-idyllic means of securing her wish, Sarah wants to protect the line of Abraham by giving her husband a son. The Hebrew midwives Shiphrah and Puah defy the Egyptian king's order to kill all male children at birth. Miriam protects her infant brother, Moses, by convincing Pharaoh's daughter to use Moses' own mother as a nursemaid. Rahab protects Joshua's spies from the king of Jericho. Bathsheba protects Solomon's promised succession to the throne of David. Deborah, Judith, and Esther engage in diplomatic and literal warfare to protect God's people from spiritual and physical harm. Even Wisdom, that divine interlocutor who is personified as "she" in both Judeo-Christian and pagan sources, seeks to protect her hearers from falling into stupidity and misfortune.

In the New Testament, the women are more nuanced in their concern for the human person; temporal protection and healing are less of a surrogate and more of an external overflow of the internal disposition. Mary of Bethany, ever at the feet of Jesus, proclaims and preserves the truth about the Messiah when she prefers to listen to Christ's words over helping her sister. Martha's faith leads to Jesus' raising Lazarus from the dead. Credit goes also to Pilate's wife, who seeks to protect Jesus from unjust condemnation. And when Mary Magdalene and her companions discover that Christ's body is missing from His tomb, they are initially distraught at the horrible thing done to the dead — a result of the desire to protect what remains of their Lord.

Illumination

Through their inclination toward protecting the integrity of the human person, the women of the Gospel and their Old Testament predecessors shed light on humanity's incomparable dignity and value. Moreover, they drive home the fact that the dignity of the human person does not come from a temporal source, nor is it affected by temporal means; human worth is measured only by divine scales.

The illumination of this dignity reveals a type of freedom: freedom from despair in times of suffering; freedom from anger and envy; freedom to live with joy and hope and holy fear that God reads the human heart and will respond with mercy and justice. Hannah's, Judith's, and Esther's prayers of thanksgiving are prime examples; the most famous exclamation of human dignity from the mouth of a woman is the Mother of God's Magnificat:

> My soul magnifies the Lord, and my spirit rejoices in God my Savior, for he has regarded the low estate of his handmaiden. For behold, henceforth all generations will call me blessed; for he who is mighty has done great things for me, and holy is his name. And his mercy is on those who fear him from generation to generation. He has shown strength with his arm, he has scattered the proud in the imagination of their hearts, he has put down the mighty from their thrones, and exalted those of low degree; he has filled the hungry with good things, and the rich he has sent empty away. He has helped his servant Israel, in remembrance of his mercy, as he spoke to our fathers, to Abraham and to his posterity for ever. (Luke 1:46–55)

The Supreme Vocation of Women

The righteous women of the Old Testament and the Gospel women also testify that by fully submitting oneself to God, the human person is capable of profound transformations. Deborah prophesies, and Judith sermonizes; both open the eyes of the people to their provocations against God and secure the opportunity for repentance, conversion, and salvation. Esther reveals Haman's plot to destroy the Hebrews, earning her people a chance to reverse their fortune and defend themselves. Susanna's silence makes room for the divine revelation of truth and the triumph of justice. Ruth and the foreign women are proof that salvation is available to all "who are blind, yet have eyes, who are deaf, yet have ears" (Isa. 43:8). By washing His feet and anointing Him with oil, Mary of Bethany not only prepares Jesus for His Passion and death but also warns us that the cost of conversion is high. And Mary Magdalene announces Christ's Resurrection—the fulfillment of the Scriptures.

Relation

While it is not always explained outright, the protective inclinations of these women and what they indicate about the nature and dignity of the human person are a living catechesis of the divine desire that created humanity: "Let us make man in our image, after our likeness" (Gen. 1:26). Humanity is inextricably bound up with God, from the beginning of time. The divine image is what sets man apart from the rest of creation, and Original Sin's brutal desecration of that image is the impetus for the entire salvation history that follows. It is one reason why the Incarnation and the christological doctrine of Jesus' dual nature are *sensible*: man, who is given a small share of the divine nature from conception, is fittingly redeemed by the Divine Son, who takes on a human nature.

The women of the Gospel and their Old Testament counterparts understand this in a visceral way, and they devote their
energies to encouraging, exhorting, and engaging humanity in
a return to its roots: rediscovering our personhood in the divine
image — in Christ. Each of them gives witness to the fact that
who we are, and what we do, *matters*. It matters to God; it matters to those who seek God with us or through us; it matters to
those who don't know God and may meet Him for the first time
in us. In the words of Judith, "Now therefore, brethren, let us
set an example to our brethren, for their lives depend upon us,
and the sanctuary and the temple and the altar rest upon us. In
spite of everything let us give thanks to the Lord our God, who
is putting us to the test as he did our forefathers" (Jth. 8:24–25).

A Woman's Mission

Perhaps the most significant thing to come from John Paul II's
consideration of the Gospel women is the title he chooses to
give them: "Guardians of the Gospel Message." It is a moniker
that seems better suited for the Mother of God, rather than
those who seek out Christ for His intervention. But in women
such as the Samaritan at the well, Martha, the Marys, and the
hemorrhaging woman — as well as the righteous Old Testament
women — John Paul II notes the consistent patterns of behavior;
he observes that womanhood appears predisposed to a particular
mission. From his observations, he concludes *Mulieris Dignitatem*
by making his determination that "God entrusts the human being to [women] in a special way."[53] He never explicitly identifies
what the "special way" is, but in his *Letter to Women*, written

---

[53] The entire quotation is introduced at the end of paragraph 30.

seventeen years after *Mulieris Dignitatem*, John Paul II continues to articulate his vision:

> For in giving themselves to others each day women fulfill their deepest vocation. Perhaps more than men, women *acknowledge the person*, because they see persons with their hearts. They see them independently of various ideological or political systems. They see others in their greatness and limitations; they try to go out to them and *help them*. In this way the basic plan of the Creator takes flesh in the history of humanity and there is constantly revealed, in the variety of vocations, that *beauty* — not merely physical, but above all spiritual — which God bestowed from the very beginning on all, and in a particular way on women.[54]

In light of the progression of John Paul II's vision of womanhood, and what is observable from our reflection on the women of Scripture, calling these women "guardians" makes sense. Women such as Judith, Ruth, Deborah, the Samaritan at the well, and Mary Magdalene — in the variety of their endeavors — promote and protect what is good and true about humanity. They stand for the full dignity of the human person and against any encroachment upon that fullness; there is no tolerance for reducing one's eternal value to a bland version that is measured in materials and moments.

This brings us full circle to John Paul II's final exhortation to women: "To you, women, falls the task of being *sentinels of the Invisible*!" Taking the parallel journey through salvation history to the time of Christ and through the development of John Paul

---

[54] *Letter to Women*, no. 12.

II's theological anthropology of women, the import of these words becomes more apparent and their significance more profound. Womanhood is endowed with the fundamental vocation to stand guard over humanity, from the individual to the communities of entire nations, and maintain the incomparable dignity and value of human life that is rooted in God's likeness in every person. This is the lived reality of the feminine genius, the fullness of feminine agency in the divine plan: that womanhood guards the person *in Christ*—human nature reconciled with God.

6

Saintly Sentinels

As the days and weeks after Mary Magdalene's discovery of Christ's empty tomb matured into centuries, the lived reality of womanhood in the divine plan continued to give witness in all its particular form and ferocity. Women from every corner of the world, and from every class and circumstance, embraced the Christian Faith; taking up the way of the sentinel, they "set the world on fire." The Church recognizes some of these women as saints. Many more women, like the radiant unnamed lady in C. S. Lewis's *The Great Divorce*, are known only to God. But all of them illustrate the lived reality of the feminine genius—of what it means, in practical terms, to be a sentinel of the Invisible. Included in this holy congregation of women are St. Cecilia, St. Catherine of Alexandria, St. Monica, St. Mary of Egypt, St. Birgitta of Sweden, St. Thérèse of Lisieux, St. Katharine Drexel, and St. Margaret of Antioch.

St. Cecilia

Personally, Emperor Severus Alexander liked the rising Christian religion. But to keep his constituents—and his advisers—placated, he maintained a neutral public stance. This allowed local Roman administrators to do with the Christians as they wished. More often than not, that meant persecution. Many Romans were horrified by the tenets of the Christian Faith; a sect founded on "principles of eternal jurisprudence" that "rejected the control of political power" and "assign[ed] faith as the guide of intellect" seemed contrary to everything that Rome stood for. And because the law favored Rome, and the Roman gods, it was easy for those who wanted an excuse to persecute Christians to find one.

The most renowned Christian to be martyred under Severus Alexander was St. Cecilia. Despite being born into an illustrious pagan family, Cecilia was encouraged in the Christian Faith from a young age. She kept the Gospels under her clothes and close to her heart at all times and frequently visited the catacombs to pray for the dead. Not realizing that their daughter vowed to remain a virgin bride for Christ, Cecilia's parents arranged for her to marry the son of another noble family, Valerian. The young man was handsome and kind; Cecilia knew that she could be happy with him but did not want to break her vow to Christ. She prayed without ceasing during the wedding and during the journey to her husband's home; while the pagan festivities raged, Cecilia "sang in the depth of her heart, and her melody was united to that of angels." When it was time to consummate the marriage, she confessed to her husband that an angel of God guarded her virginity. She warned Valerian of the angel's vengeance if her husband demanded that the marriage be consummated but said that the angel would bless him if he chose to guard his wife's integrity. Valerian asked to see the angel, as proof of her claim, and Cecilia advised him to be baptized by Pope Urban on the Appian Way — he would see her angel then. Everything passed as Cecilia said, and Valerian and Cecilia lived in chaste friendship. The couple devoted their time and fortune to supporting the poor and the growing Church. When the prefect of Rome initiated a fresh round of Christian persecutions—and forbade Christians to bury their dead—Cecilia and her husband were among those who defied the edict, interring the martyrs in the catacombs beneath the Appian Way.

Because of their prominent social standing in Roman society, word of Cecilia and Valerian's endeavors reached the prefect. Valerian was martyred first, with his brother Tiburtius. Cecilia buried them personally. Knowing her own martyrdom was imminent, she arranged for her possessions to be distributed among the poor, and her home put in trust for the Church to use as a place of worship. The prefect came for Cecilia and demanded that she sacrifice to the gods. She refused, and he locked her in her own bath house to die from heat exhaustion. Despite spending the night locked in the boiling room, Cecilia did not break a sweat. Unnerved, the prefect ordered an executioner to behead the widow. The unsteady hands of the executioner failed him: he tried three times to sever Cecilia's head but could not. He had to—by law—leave her where she was, barely alive and bathing in her own blood. She died three days later. Pope Urban buried her himself, laying her to rest in a tomb adjacent to the crypt of the popes in the Catacombs of Callixtus.[55]

---

[55] Details of St. Cecilia's life are taken from Rev. Prosper Gueranger, *Life of Saint Cecilia, Virgin and Martyr* (Philadelphia: Fetek P. Cunningham, 1866), Internet Archive, https://archive.org/stream/lifeofsaintcecil00gura/lifeofsaintcecil00gura_djvu.txt.

St. Catherine of Alexandria

The ascent of Diocletian to the role of Augustus in A.D. 284 did not bode well for Christians in the Roman Empire. Preferring the gods and the glory of the empire's past, the new caesar placed increasing restrictions on Christian freedoms before calling a general persecution in 303. Persecutions across the empire varied in intensity; some regional emperors were less enthusiastic about the draconian policies and ended their part in the persecutions as early as 306. The emperor Maximinus II was not one of them. According to the historian Eusebius, the Christians living under Maximinus's jurisdiction were subject to brutal treatment:

> Some of them, after scrapings and rackings and severest scourgings, and numberless other kinds of tortures, terrible even to hear of, were committed to the flames; some were drowned in the sea; some offered their heads bravely to those who cut them off; some died under their tortures, and others perished with hunger. And yet others were crucified; some according to the method commonly employed for malefactors; others yet more cruelly, being nailed to the cross with their heads downward, and being kept alive until they perished on the cross with hunger.[56]

One day, a beautiful young noblewoman sought an audience with the emperor: "Catherine, daughter of Constus, the governor of Alexandria." Standing before him, the young woman unleashed a blistering censure of Maximinus's policies against the Christians and a rousing defense of the Christian Faith.

---

[56] Eusebius, *Church History*, bk. 8, chap. 8, no. 2.

Equally impressed and incensed by Catherine's rhetoric, the emperor brought in his most accomplished philosophers to refute her. Their efforts backfired. Instead of leading Catherine to admit any deficiency in the Christian Faith, many of the philosophers were convinced by the young woman's apologia, and they converted and incurred immediate martyrdom. Changing tactics, Maximinus tried tempting Catherine into apostasy with an offer of marriage. She refused, claiming Christ as her only spouse. Enraged, he ordered Catherine's torture and imprisonment. When members of the emperor's inner circle visited Catherine in her cell, they, too, converted and suffered martyrdom. Maximinus then sent Catherine to the breaking wheel for execution, but the wheel broke as soon as it touched the young woman's body. The emperor settled for having her beheaded.[57]

St. Monica

Monica of Tagaste had plenty to pray about. Her husband, who took after his mother, was a temperamental pagan, prone to rage and destructive habits. He refused to allow their children to be baptized and often expressed his annoyance at Monica's devotion to prayer and charity toward the poor. To make matters worse, her eldest son, Augustine, was a lothario who embraced every philosophy save the Christian one of his mother. There was no reasoning or arguing with either man; all Monica could do was

---

[57] Details of St. Catherine's life are taken from L. Clugnet, "St. Catherine of Alexandria," *Catholic Encyclopedia*, vol. 3 (New York: Robert Appleton Company, 1908), http://www.newadvent.org/cathen/03445a.htm.

pray and live out her Christian Faith to the best of her ability. In addition to her frequent almsgiving, Monica organized a local support group for wives and mothers in difficult domestic situations.

Monica's gentle disposition and constant faith led to her husband's conversion, shortly before his death. Augustine, on the other hand, was another matter. His persistence in vice and heresy led Monica to kick him out of the house in frustration. Praying and weeping bitterly over the situation, she received a vision encouraging her to reconcile with her son. Monica pursued this reconciliation with Augustine throughout many years and over hundreds of miles. She traveled to Rome, where her son first attempted to hide from her. Upon her arrival, Monica discovered that Augustine had fled to Milan. Heartbroken but undaunted, she followed him. With the help of Ambrose, the bishop of Milan, Augustine reconciled with his mother and with the Christian Faith. Monica had the joy of seeing her son's entrance into the Church before they decided to return to Africa together. Monica died en route. As Augustine recounted in his *Confessions*, she knew there was nothing left for her in this life:

> Then said my mother, "*Son, for myself, I have no longer any pleasure in anything in this life. What I want here further, and why I am here, I know not, now that my hopes in this world are satisfied. There was indeed one thing for which I wished to tarry a little in this life, and that was that I might see you a Catholic Christian before I died. My God has exceeded this abundantly, so that I see you despising all earthly felicity, made His servant—what do I here?*"[58]

---

[58] Augustine, *Confessions*, bk. 9, chap. 10. Details of St. Monica's life are taken from H. Pope, "St. Monica," *Catholic Encyclopedia*,

St. Mary of Egypt

After fifty-three years in the same monastery, the holy monk Zosima feared he was growing arrogant in his own piety. As he later related to younger monks, "he began to be tormented with the thought that he was perfect in everything and needed no instruction from anyone." After being counseled by an angel to seek "spiritual profit" at the monastery by the River Jordan, Zosima journeyed to his new home and immersed himself in the asceticism of his desert brothers.

When it came time for the monks' traditional Lenten practice of wandering alone in the desert, Zosima went out with them "with a secret hope of finding some father who might be living there and who might be able to satisfy his thirst and longing." His hope was not in vain; after wandering for twenty days, he beheld a naked form, darkened by the sun and crowned with white hair. Pursuing the figure, he was stunned to discover that the holy one he had prayed for was a woman—*and she knew him by name.* Giving her his cloak, the monk begged the woman to tell him her story: how God worked through her and brought her to such a pure existence. Two years passed before the monk learned her name, but Zosima made sure that no one would forget it: Mary of Egypt.

In terms of drama, Mary's story and conversion rivals St. Paul's incredible tale. Impetus unknown, Mary abandoned her family at the age of twelve and traveled to the great city of Alexandria, where "I at first ruined my maidenhood and then unrestrainedly and insatiably gave myself up to sensuality.... I was like a fire of public debauch." She enjoyed the licentiousness

vol. 10 (New York: Robert Appleton Company, 1911), http://www.newadvent.org/cathen/10482a.htm.

of prostitution with such abandon that she often refused pay-
ment for her services. Seventeen years of her life were spent
"lying in filth," as she confessed to the dumbfounded monk.
One day, when Mary spied a throng of men running to the port,
seeking passage to Jerusalem for the feast of the Exaltation of
the Cross, she saw an opportunity for further debauchery and
boarded the ship. Paying for her passage with her body, Mary
reveled in "unmentionable depravity," admitting even to forcing
sex on unwilling passengers. Nothing changed upon her arrival
in Jerusalem, until the feast day. Caught up in the throng trying
to enter the church, she found herself unable to pass through
the door:

> I had at last squeezed through with great difficulty almost
> to the entrance of the temple, from which the lifegiving
> Tree of the Cross was being shown to the people. But
> when I trod on the doorstep which everyone passed, I
> was stopped by some force which prevented my entering.
> Meanwhile I was brushed aside by the crowd and found
> myself standing alone in the porch. Thinking that this
> had happened because of my woman's weakness, I again
> began to work my way into the crowd, trying to elbow
> myself forward. But in vain I struggled. Again my feet
> trod on the doorstep over which others were entering the
> church without encountering any obstacle. I alone seemed
> to remain unaccepted by the church. It was as if there
> was a detachment of soldiers standing there to oppose my
> entrance. Once again I was excluded by the same mighty
> force, and again I stood in the porch. Having repeated my
> attempt three or four times, at last I felt exhausted and
> had no more strength to push and to be pushed, so I went

aside and stood in a corner of the porch. And only then with great difficulty it began to dawn on me, and I began to understand the reason why I was prevented from being admitted to see the lifegiving Cross. The word of salvation gently touched the eyes of my heart and revealed to me that it was my unclean life which barred the entrance to me. I began to weep and lament and beat my breast, and to sigh from the depths of my heart.

Seeing an icon of the Theotokos outside the church, Mary pleaded for forgiveness. She vowed to the Blessed Mother that if she was allowed to see the Holy Cross of Christ, she would cease her wicked life and start a new one wherever the Mother of God wanted her to go. Mary was granted entrance into the church, where she fell prostrate before the Cross. After her veneration, she returned to the icon and heard a voice telling her, "If you cross the Jordan, you will find glorious rest." Buying three loaves of bread with money given to her by a passing stranger, Mary traveled to the Jordan and made her way into the desert. For forty-seven years, she battled temptations and clung to God as her only companion, until the day Zosima found her. After regaling the monk with her tale, she made a single request: that he return in one year—precisely—with the Holy Eucharist so that she may receive Christ. The monk honored her request, not knowing that shortly after receiving the sacrament of Holy Communion, Mary was received into the Beatific Vision.[59]

[59] The story of Mary's life and her encounter with the monk Zosima is recounted in her *Vita*, written by St. Sophronius in the seventh century; it can be found on the website of Saint Mary of Egypt Orthodox Church, https://www.stmaryofegypt.org/files/library/life.htm.

St. Birgitta of Sweden

The early life of St. Birgitta sounds like a fairy tale. Born around 1303 to an illustrious knight and a relative of the royal House of Bjälbo, little Birgitta grew up cocooned in love, comfort, and a pious devotion to the Christian Faith. This lifestyle remained with the young woman into her marriage. Betrothed at a very young age, Birgitta's husband, Ulf, was equally devout; they made a happy life together with their eight children. As her family grew, so did Birgitta's renown as a pious, charitable matron. She was devoted to helping the poor and the sick, especially unwed mothers and their children. And when she was chosen to be the queen of Sweden's lady-in-waiting, Birgitta used the opportunity to be a voice of moral reason in the royal court. These qualities earned her many friends among the clerics and scholars of Sweden.

Ulf's death in 1344 hit Birgitta hard. After allowing herself time to mourn, Birgitta put her affairs in order and devoted her widowhood to the religious life as a Franciscan tertiary, rooting it in ascetic practices. During this time, she formulated the idea for a new religious community. In 1350, she traveled to Rome to petition for the Church's approval of the order. Because this was during the Avignon Papacy, twenty years passed before a pope resided in Rome long enough to give the approval. Birgitta did not sit idle: Rome's poor and sick benefited from her generous heart; she advocated for peace between the city-states; she urged the Church to embrace ecclesial reforms; she exhorted everyone to embrace spiritual renewal and moral improvement. She also entreated the pope to return to Rome.

Unlike her contemporary, St. Catherine of Siena, Birgitta did not live to see the fruits of her labors. She died without seeing peace between the Italian nobility, the end of the Avignon

Papacy, and the flourishing of her order. In a sense, Birgitta is the "Patroness of Failures."[60]

St. Thérèse of Lisieux

Thérèse Martin was the precocious youngest child of Louis and Zélie Martin. She was happy, affectionate, playful, and prone to throw tantrums when denied her desires; her father nicknamed her the "little queen." Thérèse's demeanor changed with the death of her mother, when she was four years old. The child became nervous and quiet, requiring more gentle attention from her father and sisters—which they gave her in abundance. The family's Catholic Faith was a source of comfort for Thérèse, and from a young age the child was drawn to contemplation and the sacraments. School was a miserable experience for her: intellectually gifted, Thérèse was bored and bullied. When her sister Pauline entered the Carmelite monastery, nine-year-old Thérèse broke down with a terrible unknown illness. She suffered from headaches, fevers, tremors, and hallucinations for a year; the doctors were baffled and unable to help her. Thérèse eventually recovered, telling her family that a vision of the statue of Mary by her bed "radiating love and kindness" was her cure. It was during her illness that Thérèse became determined to enter the Carmelite monastery and devote her life to Christ. She was rejected twice—because of her young age—but her

---

[60] Details of St. Birgitta's life are taken from "St. Bridget of Sweden," Catholic Online, https://www.catholic.org/saints/saint.php?saint_id=264; *Encyclopedia of World Biographies*, s.v. "St. Bridget of Sweden," https://www.notablebiographies.com/supp/Supplement-A-Bu-and-Obituaries/Bridget-of-Sweden.html.

determination won out. She entered the monastery four months after her fifteenth birthday.

Before she entered the monastery, and after years of internal struggle, Thérèse received an epiphany that helped her regain her childhood joy: "My heart was filled with charity. I forgot myself to please others and, in doing so, became happy myself." This became the cornerstone of Thérèse's life as a cloister. Whatever she did, she did with great love. She performed her duties cheerfully, she smiled at those who mocked her and criticized her for her slowness, and she held her tongue at the petty annoyances of communal life.

Thérèse died of tuberculosis at the age of twenty-four, leaving behind an autobiography, numerous letters, poems, and original prayers.[61]

St. Katharine Drexel

The late nineteenth and early twentieth century was a turbulent period of transition for the United States and her people, especially America's minority populations. The Thirteenth Amendment of 1865 and the Civil Rights Act of 1866 improved the legal landscape for African Americans but did not eliminate the deep-seated bigotry and antagonism that assaulted them daily. It would be another century before the eradication of racial discrimination was made a provision of the Thirteenth Amendment. The Native American populations did not even have the law on their side. The early nineteenth century saw

---

[61] Details of St. Thérèse's life are taken from "The Story of St. Thérèse's Life," Society of the Little Flower, https://www.little-flower.org/therese/life-story/.

the loss of native lands east of the Mississippi River and the creation of reservations, and between 1887 and 1940 Native Americans lost another 106 million acres to American expansion. Citizenship and sporadic voting rights were not granted until 1924, fifty-four years after African American men were allowed to vote, and four years after African American women received voting rights.

In 1881, Helen Hunt Jackson wrote *A Century of Dishonor*, detailing the unjust experience of Native Americans in the United States. The book had a profound effect on twenty-three-year-old Philadelphia socialite Katharine Drexel. Sensitive to the sufferings of Philadelphia's poor and African American communities, the history of the Native American people in America struck a nerve in the devout Catholic. When she and her family traveled across the western United States a few years later and saw the Native Americans' lived reality with her own eyes, Katharine decided to focus her energies on supporting poor minority communities throughout the country. At first, she focused on donating large portions of her family wealth to various missions and schools in impoverished areas. During a visit to Wyoming, Katharine realized that many of the missions were understaffed. She traveled to Rome, hoping that Pope Leo XII would agree to send her more missionaries. The Holy Father countered her request with the suggestion that she become a missionary. Already considering a vocation to religious life, she took the pope's words to heart, choosing a life lived for God and the marginalized over the comforts of high society.

"Mother" Katharine founded the Sisters of the Blessed Sacrament, an order of nuns dedicated to providing poor Native American and African American communities with education and faith formation. Under Katharine's guidance, 145 missions, 50 schools for African Americans, and 12 schools for Native Americans were established across the American South and West, despite sometimes-violent supremacist opposition. Katharine remained a formidable advocate for social justice until a heart attack forced her to retire as the order's superior. She died twenty years later, at the age of ninety-six.[62]

St. Margaret of Antioch

Margaret of Antioch was a late-third- or early-fourth-century martyr; little else is known about her as a historical person. As a myth, she is an ode to the fierce magnificence of womanhood in communion with Christ. According to *The Golden Legend*, Margaret was tortured and imprisoned for her faith. During her incarceration, the devil appeared to her—first as a dragon, then as a man. The dragon devoured Margaret, but when she made the Sign of the Cross, his belly burst open and released her, whole and unharmed. The man tried to convince Margaret to stop bothering him. Without hesitation, Margaret "caught him by the head and threw him to the ground, and set her right foot on his neck, saying: 'Lie still, you fiend, under the foot of a woman.'"[63]

---

[62] Details of St. Katharine's life are taken from "St. Katharine Drexel," Catholic News Agency, https://www.catholicnewsagency.com/saint/st-katharine-drexel-166; "St. Katharine Drexel," Philanthropy Roundtable, https://www.philanthropyroundtable.org/almanac/people/hall-of-fame/detail/st.-katharine-drexel.

[63] Jacobus de Voragine, "The Legend of St. Margaret," in *The Golden Legend*.

Reading between the Lives

Sts. Cecilia, Catherine, Monica, Mary, Birgitta, Thérèse, Katharine, and Margaret are joined by many more beloved female saints: Hildegard of Bingen, Elizabeth of Hungary, Josephine Bakhita, Rose of Lima, Teresa of Avila, Agnes, Lucy, Edith Stein, Elizabeth Ann Seton, Joan of Arc, Brigid of Ireland, Philomena, Scholastica, Olga; the list goes on. It is not difficult to see the parallels and similarities between these women and those who precede them in the Old Testament and the Gospels. The same tendencies toward protection, illumination, and relation are as potent in Monica and Katharine as they are in Judith and Ruth. Through prayer, frequent reception of the sacraments, and the unconditional willingness to give one's life, talent, and treasure to the Body of Christ, the Church's female saints echo Mary of Bethany's desire to remain at the feet of Jesus, and the Old Testament women's unwavering personal integrity in the Mosaic law.

The dignity and vocation of womanhood shine even more when we pause to contemplate the lives of these holy women in tandem with their male contemporaries. Consider: St. Cecilia and St. Irenaeus lived and died within thirty years of each other; St. Monica and St. Ambrose were friends; St. Mary of Egypt was in the desert while St. John Chrysostom was earning his nickname "Golden Mouth"; St. Catherine of Alexandria was martyred two years after St. Valentine; St. Birgitta's time in Rome coincided with the formative years of St. John Nepomucene; St. Thérèse of Lisieux found her Little Way while St. Damien de Veuster was on the Hawaiian island of Molokai as the pastor and doctor for the lepers at the Kalaupapa settlement; St. Katharine Drexel was busy founding schools and missions when St. Maximilian Kolbe entered a Franciscan seminary in 1907. The contemporaries of each century offer resounding witness to the Church's universal call to communion with Christ and a life of witness, but, like the complementary creation accounts in Genesis, women and men respond to this call in their own distinct ways.

St. Cecilia guarded her virginity, vowing to give herself only to Christ; St. Irenaeus defended the early Church's understanding of Christ. St. Monica entrusted herself and her son to God's mercy and love, flooding Heaven with her tears and prayers for her family's conversion and salvation; St. Ambrose's ability to "speak the truth, and speak it well, judiciously, pointedly, and with beauty and power of expression"[64] made him a forceful counterpoint to the Arian heresy. Using herself as a cautionary example, St. Mary gave witness to the incomparable value of conversion, salvation, and a moral life; St. John Chrysostom was called "Golden Mouth" for his practical and eloquent wisdom on the Scriptures and morality. St. Birgitta refused to give up on her order, on the return of the papacy to Rome, on caring for the poor, or on working for peace; St. John Nepomucene was martyred for refusing to break the seal of confession. St. Thérèse of Lisieux observed Christ's love in daily matters; St. Damien observed Christ's love in desperate matters. St. Katharine Drexel endured threats and violence to bring the Catholic Faith to the marginalized of American society; St. Maximilian Kolbe endured violence to bring the sacraments to prisoners in Auschwitz.

The tendency of the female saints to advocate for personal dignity, integrity, and conformity to the person and message of Christ reinforces our understanding of womanhood as guardian of the person *in Christ*. The female saints are concerned about facilitating a radical and intimate encounter with Christ; the

---

[64] Augustine, *On Christian Doctrine*, bk. 4, chap. 21.

works of mercy are their weapons. But from the brief sample of male saints, a discrete tendency emerges: the tendency to advocate for everything that pertains to Christ Himself. They preach, they defend doctrine, they ensure access to the sacraments—where Christ is truly present—and they tend to the people entrusted to them, just like Christ the Good Shepherd. They are true to the charism of the sacrament of Holy Orders: to act *in persona Christi capitis.* The same appears true for the saintly men who were called to marriage, such as Sts. Thomas More and Louis Martin. This suggests that the vocation of manhood in the divine plan, complementary to the vocation of womanhood, is to guard the person *of Christ.*

From this representative segment of male and female saints, it is clear that these vocations complement, rather than conflict with, each other. Traditionally the Church identifies, explains, and advocates for this complementarity with language that is common to every discipline of human knowledge: motherhood, fatherhood, and virginity. These labels and their connotations cause fierce debate between the evolving sciences and culture, and the perennial teachings of the Church—especially in regard to the subject of women. But in the primordial qualities of virginity, motherhood, and fatherhood, the Church sees the infinite potential and dignity of the human person, distinguished by sex. Here, too, an understanding of women as sentinels of the Invisible, illuminated by the example of the Church's holy women throughout salvation history, offers us a better sense of what the Church communicates about the "particular dimensions"[65] of womanhood.

---

[65] *Mulieris Dignitatem*, no. 17.

7

Motherhood

To understand the mind of the Church on motherhood, we need
to revisit the Theotokos. Mary's role as the Mother of God comes
with no small amount of controversy. The Council of Ephesus
was called to settle definitively the issue of whether God could
be "born," and whether Mary should be called "Christ bearer"
or "God bearer." The author of the controversy, Nestorius, could
not reconcile how Jesus, who had an obvious human nature, did
not also have the inheritance of sin that all human natures are
bound to inherit from Adam. He failed to account for what the
Church Fathers already insinuated as fact in their writings: that
Mary herself was preserved, from the moment of her conception,
from all sin. She is immaculate; free from the stain of Original Sin
and unburdened by actual, personal sin. This belief continued,
with few challenges,[66] to be an integral part of Catholic Tradition until its solemn confirmation as dogma in 1854. Tandem to

---

[66] Surprisingly, the strongest objections to Mary's Immaculate
Conception came from the giants of medieval theology: Sts.
Bernard of Clairvaux (d. 1153), Thomas Aquinas (d. 1274),
and Bonaventure (d. 1274). Aquinas's opinion, especially, was
held in such high esteem that the Council of Trent (1545–1563)
refused to get involved in the matter.

the belief in Mary's sinlessness is that of her perpetual virginity. Scripture affirms that Mary was a virgin when she conceived Jesus, and by the third century, the Church Fathers formed a general consensus that her virginity was of a nature equal to her innocence: complete and permanent. Though never solemnly confirmed as dogma, Mary's perpetual virginity is consistently upheld as part of the Church teaching that all the faithful are bound to believe. As early as the Second Ecumenical Council of Constantinople (553), those who did not confess that Christ was born of "Mary, Mother of God and always a virgin" were considered anathema.

Mary, in her role as Theotokos, is "wholly exceptional and unique."[67] By the grace of God, she is both virgin and mother; human, yet free from sin. But, as John Paul II points out, God does not change the nature of a person with His grace—He perfects what already exists.[68] Because Mary's "virginity and motherhood co-exist in her: they do not mutually exclude each other or place limits on each other,"[69] the Church recognizes that the Mother of God marks an important shift in the entire concept of motherhood.

Motherhood as a Mode

Motherhood is not merely something that a woman does. It is first and foremost an internal disposition of the female personality. Christian tradition holds that God created woman with the intention of entrusting the human person to her care, endowing

[67] *Redemptoris Mater*, no. 9.
[68] *Mulieris Dignitatem*, no. 5.
[69] Ibid., no. 17.

her with the capabilities and inclinations necessary to execute this divine service:

> "It is not good for man to be alone: let us make him a helper fit for him" (Gen. 2:18). God entrusted the human being to woman. Certainly, every human being is entrusted to each and every other human being, but in a special way the human being is entrusted to woman, precisely because the woman in virtue of her special experience of motherhood is seen to have a *specific sensitivity* towards the human person and all that constitutes the individual's true welfare, beginning with the fundamental value of life.[70]

This "specific sensitivity" in the words of the world often translates to greater emotional empathy,[71] heightened emotional intelligence,[72] and the conventional wisdom about women's

---

[70] *Christifidelis Laici*, no. 51.

[71] As indicated by a growing number of longitudinal psychological studies, such as M. Vincenta Mestre Escriva, Paula Samper Garcia, M. Dolores Frias Navarro, and Ana Maria Tur Porcar, "Are Women More Empathetic Than Men?: A Longitudinal Study in Adolescence," *Spanish Journal of Psychology* 12, no. 1 (2009): 76–83, https://www.cambridge.org/core/journals/spanish-journal-of-psychology/article/are-women-more-empathetic-than-men-a-longitudinal-study-in-adolescence/8900C6ABC5BE52BCE657367A8516E48D.

[72] Also indicated by a number of studies, such as Marc A. Brackett, Susan E. Rivers, Sara Shiffman, Nicole Lerner, and Peter Salovey, "Relating Emotional Abilities to Social Functioning: A Comparison of Self-Report and Performance Measures of Emotional Intelligence," *Journal of Personality and Social Psychology* 91, no. 4 (2006): 780–795, https://psycnet.apa.org/doiLanding?doi=10.1037%2F0022-3514.91.4.780.

intuition. Regardless of how it is termed, the Church affirms that every woman is created with this disposition, in the anticipation that she will take up her commission and act on it. But the Church also acknowledges that this disposition is not magic. It must be tended and cultivated; without attention, the potential remains dormant or becomes stunted.

When it is encouraged, the maternal disposition manifests itself in two ways: as spiritual motherhood and as physical motherhood. Physical motherhood, as the name implies, is the biological process where a woman grows a child in her womb. Spiritual motherhood is concerned with the "personal-ethical"[73] dimension of the human person. It cultivates and protects the needs of the whole person: physical, mental, emotional, and spiritual. Ideally, spiritual and physical motherhood are inseparable, both operating as one, but they are not mutually dependent. Spiritual motherhood does not depend on the fact of physical motherhood in order to act. The Old Testament Hebrews had Deborah and Judith as spiritual mothers; we have godmothers, beloved "aunties," and many more women who pour out their maternal affections on those of us who are not their children. And while physical motherhood suffers when separated from spiritual motherhood, a woman does not need to be a spiritual mother in order to get pregnant.

Mary, as the Mother of God, exemplifies the ideal. She gave Jesus flesh from her own flesh, and blood from her own blood. She kept Him in her home, fed Him, clothed Him, and saw that He received instruction in the law and in a trade. She supported His ministry and remained by His side, even when it was at the foot of the Cross. And when Jesus entrusted Mary to the beloved

[73] *Mulieris Dignitatem*, no. 19.

disciple John, and him to her (John 19:26–27) before His death, she became the Mother of the Church—*our* mother, in the order of grace and according to the Spirit. She extended her maternal care over the entire world, adopting every person, in every era, as her own child. And though Mary's spiritual motherhood, in the sense of her being Mother of the Church, follows the fact of her physical motherhood, the Church is quick to point out that she "conceived this Son in her mind before she conceived him in her womb."[74] Mary's motherhood starts in the spirit, with her openness to life, takes definite shape within her body, and continues indefinitely as a motherhood of adoption.

In this way, the Theotokos guides the Church toward a radical perspective on the nature of motherhood. She affirms that it is primarily a spiritual mode of existence, not a biological process. While physicality is a crucial aspect of motherhood, the activity of motherhood includes much more than the development of genetic material into a discernible human form, because the human person is much more than just a form. The human person is a soul and a body, a mind and a will. Consequently, the purpose of motherhood is primarily spiritual in nature. It is tasked with the preservation and cultivation of what makes the human experience authentically human: a person, in his or her totality, conformed to God's divine likeness and in covenant with Him, through Christ.

Motherhood as a Vocation

In order for one thing to conform to another, the former must be shaped in a way that fits the form of the latter. Sometimes the

---

[74] *Redemptoris Mater*, no. 13.

first thing is flexible, molding itself to the other form without compromising its own integrity, like pouring a quart of water into a jug and then into an aquarium. More often it is fixed, made with a specific end in mind and limited in scope and ability outside the bounds of that end. A random piece from one jigsaw puzzle would not fit any other puzzle. Barring the wildly imaginative ideas of a small child, that lone piece has no purpose to speak of without its companion pieces. Motherhood is somewhere in between the two. It has to have a certain rigidity because it is directing a solid, concrete human being toward an immutable God. At the same time, it must be somewhat flexible because the human person is not homogenous and the immutable God is not visible. To balance these variables, Christian tradition roots motherhood in the same constant that it does personhood: the love of God.

When St. John the Apostle said that "God is love" (1 John 4:8), he meant that literally. Love is essential to God's nature. Thus, St. Augustine devised his famous love analogy to explain the relationship between the Persons of the Blessed Trinity: the Father eternally gives love, the Son eternally receives love, and the Holy Spirit is the love that is given and received; together they pour that love into the world. All of this takes place within God's unity, neither diminishing His oneness nor being diminished by it. The paradox of unity and relation that is God's life is inscribed in the human person: it is the divine likeness in which man was made and by which man discovers the fullness of the human experience. Motherhood is the way that woman manifests the divine likeness in herself and brings it out in others. It has the flexibility of being spiritual and physical, giving woman a wide range of opportunities to be a mother to others. But to ensure that it authentically reflects God's love and leads the human person to a true understanding of what it means to be human, motherhood must operate within God's logic. It has to give an accurate form to His invisible reality. This is where the vocations of marriage and consecrated virginity come in.

The Church holds that "marriage and virginity or celibacy are two ways of expressing and living the one mystery of the covenant of God with His people,"[75] with the covenant being an extension of the trinitarian communion of Persons. The covenant is a relationship of gift: the gift of one person to another, and the gift of the other back to that one. God gave Himself to us, and we were created to give ourselves back to Him. We were also created to give ourselves to one another, with the first instance of this being the spousal union of man and woman. The Church calls Marriage the "primordial sacrament" for this reason: the union of man and woman is the principal witness of the trinitarian mystery in the human experience. Christ raised it to a sacrament in the strict sense precisely because the reciprocal giving between spouses and the potential overflowing of their union into new life is as complete an analogy for God's activity as we have at our disposal.

Consecrated virginity is a subsequent, but more perfect, relationship of gift. It relinquishes the right to a spousal union with another person in order to unite oneself wholly to God:

> Women, called from the very "beginning" to be loved and to love, in a vocation to virginity *find Christ* first of all as the Redeemer who "loved until the end" through his total gift of self; *and they respond to this gift with a "sincere gift"* of their whole lives. They thus give themselves to

---

[75] *Familiaris Consortio*, no. 16.

the divine Spouse, and this personal gift tends to union, which is properly spiritual in character. Through the Holy Spirit's action a woman becomes "one spirit" with Christ the Spouse (cf. 1 Cor. 6:17).[76]

In the early years of the Church, many women embraced Christ as their betrothed and lived in the world as chaste brides. St. Margaret of Antioch and St. Agnes of Rome are well-known examples, as is St. Ambrose's sister, St. Marcellina, for whom he wrote Concerning Virgins (A.D. 377). Some of these virgins formed informal communities; when the monastic orders rose in prominence and popularity, so did discrete orders for women. By the ninth century, the Church recognized four groups of women who avowed themselves to God alone: consecrated virgins, nuns and sisters professed to a religious order, deaconesses,[77] and the order of widows. Over time, the role of deaconess became defunct and the order of widows faded into obscurity, leaving life in religious orders and consecrated virginity as the forms for women publicly to dedicate their lives to God alone.

Both vocations offer a framework for motherhood to operate with at least a minimum standard of assurance that it gives an accurate account of God's life and remains a cooperative activity with Him. Within marriage, motherhood mirrors God's eternal relation: communion between spouses leads to generative

---

[76] Mulieris Dignitatem, no. 20.

[77] It is unclear whether deaconesses were widows or women married to deacons and bound by the same vows of chastity as their husbands, but the general consensus is that deaconesses served a supportive role in the life of the Church that was not equal to priests or male deacons. For instance, deaconesses are thought to have helped women during a full-submersion Baptism, in order to maintain proper decorum during the sacrament.

abundance, which leads to more communion and abundance, and more, and more, until the whole world is united by the bonds of fraternity that are first formed within the family. This is no mere reproductive boon; it is the nucleus from which the full expression of human creativity in the world comes to life. From the abundance of generations comes a corresponding abundance of art, of music, of food, and of literature: an outpouring of self into sensual mediums that invite dialogue and relationship with another. And within consecrated virginity, motherhood explicitly affirms the oneness of God. As God is the Father of all, so, too, can a woman be a mother to all; a spiritual mother does not need a child from her own body, because her children belong to the Body of Christ.

These things, like the maternal disposition, are not magic. Entering into the sacrament of Marriage or taking public vows as a virgin, a sister, or a nun does not mean that a woman instantly becomes perfect: neither as a person, nor as a spouse, nor as a mother. Neither does it automatically reveal the divine image in its fullness. A woman must still choose to conform herself to God—to fit within the shape of His love in the ordinary circumstances of everyday life. The fiat of the Theotokos is meant to become every woman's yes: "Here I am, the servant of the Lord; let it be with me according to your word."

8

Why the Serpent Went for the Woman First

The fallen angel, seething and restless, took the form of a serpent and entered the garden. Humbling himself for the desolation of mankind, he sought out the woman. Plying her with pure sophistry, he looked on as the woman took his bait, ate the forbidden fruit, and spurred her man to partake of it. He watched as the knowledge of good and evil washed over them, opening their eyes to sin and shame; he watched them flee in terror at the sound of the Lord. And, with fitting irony, he received his just punishment: ultimate defeat at the hands of his victims.

A thought-provoking question lurks in the background of man's Fall from Original Innocence: Why did the serpent seek out the woman, and not the man, to provoke human damnation?

A number of answers may come to mind, ones that presume the vulnerability of the female personality, but all of them insufficiently consider the natural and supernatural endowments of womanhood in Original Innocence. Woman was not the weak link in the chain or the easy domino to topple. And it is impossible to know how much supernatural knowledge the devil retained after his own fall, and whether his decision was influenced by whatever knowledge he had. But it is clear by the devil's first addressing the woman and securing her participation in the Fall of man that she possessed significant agency and influence — simply by the virtue of her womanhood.

Without directly addressing this question, the Church, from her earliest days, sought to understand Eve's significance and what it indicated for the nature and dignity of womanhood. This is done primarily through a reflection on the comparative relationship between Eve and Jesus' mother. Mary is "the new Eve,"[78] and the antithesis between her and Eve is rooted in fidelity:

> And even as [Eve] ... having become disobedient, was made the cause of death, both to herself and to the entire race; so also did Mary ... by yielding obedience, become the cause of salvation, both to herself and the whole human race ... so that the former ties be cancelled by the latter, that the latter may set the former again at liberty.[79]

The antithetical relationship between Eve and Mary has many layers of meaning to it. The first layer addresses the circumstances and the consequences surrounding each woman's decision to obey or disobey God, as we see in the quotation above. Underneath that layer we see that the disobedience of one and the obedience of the other indicate a deeper personal

[78] Justin Martyr is considered one of the first to draw the comparison, in his *Dialogue with Trypho*.
[79] Irenaeus, *Against Heresies*, bk. 3, chap. 22.

disposition. Mary's entire demeanor during her encounter with the archangel Gabriel, poured out in its fullness through the words of her fiat, speaks of an obedience that is born of love. She embodies the fullness of the First Commandment: to love God with one's whole heart, soul, and might. Eve's disposition lacks this fullness. She does not need the Ten Commandments to know the natural order of things; the infusion of natural and supernatural knowledge endows her with the necessary understanding to thrive in cooperation with God's will. Yet the love she has for God is eclipsed by the reasonable-sounding poison coming from the serpent.

Underneath these layers, we find the central force of the Eve-Mary relationship. It is composed of two parts. The first is a simple premise: Eve and Mary are endowed with the capacity to direct the course of human development in all its dimensions. Eve is known as our mother according to nature, giving life — and death — to the human family. Mary, on the other hand, is our mother according to grace, facilitating our eternal, supernatural life through her Son.

The second part is logically inferred by the first: as representatives of womanhood, *which is a particular way of being human*, the endowment of agency over human development is both revealed and confirmed as an essential aspect of the female person. Eve, simply by the fact of her creation, helped Adam to develop an understanding of himself, and the nature of the human person generally, in a way that was impossible during his original solitude. And Mary, in cooperation with her Son, designated the time and the manner in which Christ was first to reveal Himself to the world — at the wedding feast in Cana.

The Supreme Vocation of Women

Women's Agency in the Order of Love

With Eve and Mary's relationship, we are reminded of the immutable truth that man is made in God's image and likeness. Eve's
agency is present from her "beginning," as is Mary's. This is not
a coincidence. It is an indication of how God desires to reveal
Himself through the female person—a trace of the Trinity in
womanhood. Neither is it a coincidence that this agency is the
one that the serpent chose to manipulate. Whether he meant
it or not, in his endeavor to pervert Eve, the serpent confirmed
what is precious about her, and womanhood as a whole: her place
in the order of love.

"God is love" (1 John 4:8). The order of love sets the conditions for man to reflect authentically the image and likeness
of God in the world of created beings. The order has two components: love of God and love of neighbor as oneself (Matt.
22:37–39). These components have a necessary complementarity
to them, to which Scripture frequently alludes:

> For as there are two commandments on which hang all
> the Law and the prophets, love of God and love of our
> neighbor; not without cause the Scripture mostly puts
> one for both: whether it be of God only, as in that text,
> "*For we know that all things work together for good to them
> that love God*" ... because he who loves God must both
> needs to do what God has commanded, and loves Him
> in just such proportion as he does so; therefore he must
> needs love his neighbor, because God has commanded it:
> or whether it be that Scripture only mentions the love of
> our neighbor, as in the text, "*Bear one another's burdens,
> and so fulfill the law of Christ*" ... he who loves his neighbor
> must needs also love above all else love itself.... But "God

is love; and he that dwells in love, dwells in God." Therefore
he must needs above all else love God.[80]

It sounds self-evident, but three things are required for the
order of love to be possible: God, Self, and an Other, as the
neighbor. Self cannot love God if God doesn't exist, any more
than Self can love a nonexistent Other. Neither can Self reflect
"the intimate life of God himself, the life of the Trinity,"[81] if the
two loves are not reconciled to each other in his or her own
person. God is eternally giving and receiving Himself in love, to
the extent that that love eternally bursts forth in creativity; there
is no active distinction between the reciprocal gift of love and
its creative fruits. Recalling the creation story in Genesis 2, we
know that man spent some time in solitude before the creation
of woman. In these moments, man is Self. And while he is able
to live in communion with God, something is missing: "God
said, 'It is not good that the man should be alone; I will make
him a helper fit for him'" (Gen. 2:18). This is the first explicit
recognition of what constitutes the image of God in man. Man
requires an Other in order to be fully himself and to fully reflect
the life of the Trinity placed within him. Self needs his neighbor.
This is where woman comes in.

John Paul II observed that "in God's eternal plan, woman is
the one in whom the order of love in the created world of persons
takes first root."[82] She is the primordial neighbor—Self's first
Other. Man needs only to see her in order to understand the full
force of having a "helper fit for him." "This at last is bone of my
bones and flesh of my flesh; she shall be called Woman, because

[80] Augustine, *On the Trinity*, bk. 8, chap. 7, no. 10.
[81] *Mulieris Dignitatem*, no. 29.
[82] Ibid.

she was taken out of Man" (Gen. 2:18, 23). John Paul II devotes a significant amount of time in his *Theology of the Body* to the consideration of what this passage of Genesis indicates for the nature and the value of the human person, but what matters here is the fact that the themes of complementarity, reciprocity, the person as gift, and inherent personal dignity are manifest precisely because woman's existence reveals them. Woman enables man—as male and female—to act as both Self and Other in the world, making visible God's invisible reality. In this way, womanhood is set up as the progenitor and the standard for the human person's love of neighbor in the world. As a result, woman has a decisive role in the orientation of the human person toward the virtue of justice.

Justice is unique among the cardinal virtues because it is always and everywhere directed toward an Other. Unlike prudence, temperance, and fortitude, which regulate the development of Self, justice regulates how Self is supposed to protect and provide for the authentic development of the Other, in light of that Other's nature. In the context of persons, justice has two dimensions: personal-moral and social-legal. It is notable that the personal-moral dimension takes primacy of place, introduced immediately in the Genesis account of creation. Like the order of love, justice toward God comes first. Man receives one instruction, to abstain from the fruit of a single tree, with the expectation that man will observe the rule with the proper obedience due God, *because of who God is*. And, as with the order of love, woman is central to the establishment of moral justice within the community of human persons. At the moment of woman's creation, man acknowledges his Other in the fullness of her humanity, her sameness ("bone of my bones"), and her distinction ("she shall be called Woman"), understanding that the humanity of his Other is a great good for him ("at last"). Woman, in turn, acknowledges man as her Other, accepting and uniting herself to the fullness of his humanity in all of its sameness and distinction. Her participation in this exchange sets the foundation for personal-moral justice—the proclamation of the human person as *good* and worthy of love—and informs the conditions on which society must build itself. To this end, womanhood is imbued with particular responsibilities: "the task of *bringing full dignity to the conjugal life and to motherhood* . . . [and] the task of *assuring the moral dimension of culture*, the dimension, namely of *a culture worthy of the person*, of an individual yet social life."[83]

Through a Glass, Darkly

Herein lies the answer to our question "Why did the serpent choose the woman?" As the primordial neighbor and progenitor of the order of love in the world, she was supposed to be the foundation on which humanity built a just society. The serpent frustrated this foundation by manipulating woman's agency, turning her strength into her weakness. He appealed to her innate desire to be a good neighbor and to share the good things of the garden with her man: "[Seeing] that the tree was good for food, and that it was a delight to the eyes, and that the tree was to be desired to make one wise, she took of its fruit and ate; and she also gave some to her husband, and he ate" (Gen. 3:6). By this small act, woman upends the order of love. Her love for God is subsumed by her love for her neighbor. But God, as the source of true justice, hands down a fitting punishment for woman's transgression: "I will greatly multiply your pain in childbearing;

[83] *Christifidelis Laici*, no. 51.

in pain you shall bring forth children, yet your desire shall be for your husband, and he shall rule over you" (Gen. 3:16). She is destined to fulfill her role in the order of love with much suffering and frustration; woman's strength is confirmed as her cross. Even before her sentence is pronounced, God promises that woman will participate in her own salvation—that her agency remains extant and necessary—but under the weight of sin, this agency is now burdened by a morass of confused priorities and distorted motives.[84]

The consequences of the serpent's machinations are numerous and binding on every person. Our wills are weak, and our minds are darkened; "we are looking at a confused reflection in a mirror" (see 1 Cor. 13:12). Nothing is murkier to us than the order of love and the divine image to which it is supposed to conform. Our sense of Other is no longer intrinsic to our sense of Self; we are isolated from our neighbor. We are led to the same question that the lawyer posed to Christ, "And who is my neighbor?" (Luke 10:29), with the same intention of self-justification. Our Other becomes an "other," a superfluous object of desire or antagonism in relation to our path toward self-realization. And as much as we champion self-sufficiency and independence as the ideal mode of the person in the modern world, the desire and manifest struggles to define, develop, and maintain good relationships belie these boasts. The loss of grace untethered us from the reality of the human experience, but because God's likeness is imbedded in us like spiritual DNA, we find ourselves in a tension of desires. We

---

[84] This fact refers to the general condition of womanhood and should not be viewed as a contradiction of the Church's doctrine on Mary's Immaculate Conception and perpetual virginity, which are alluded to in the Protoevangelium of Genesis 3:15.

desperately seek our original inheritance—identity, relationship with God and others, and the freedom to express the goodness of our created dignity—but we are incapable of discerning what these things truly are.

9

A House Divided against Itself

The American feminist movement was born with help from the mother of monsters. Mary Wollstonecraft published *A Vindication of the Rights of Woman: With Strictures on Political and Moral Subjects* in 1792, advocating for a woman's right to a formal education and equality in the moral and political spheres of society. Her treatise influenced the terms of the Declaration of Sentiments, written at the Seneca Falls Convention in 1848. The convention passed judgment on society's oppression of women, enumerating its offenses:

> The history of mankind is a history of repeated injuries and usurpations on the part of man toward woman, having in direct object the establishment of an absolute tyranny over her. To prove this, let facts be submitted to a candid world.... He has withheld her from rights which are given to the most ignorant and degraded men — both natives and foreigners.... He has made her morally, an irresponsible being, as she can commit many crimes with impunity, provided they be done in the presence of her husband. In the covenant of marriage, she is compelled to promise obedience to her husband, he becoming, to

all intents and purposes, her master—the law giving him power to deprive her of her liberty, and to administer chastisement.... He has denied her the facilities for obtaining a thorough education—all colleges being closed against her.... He has created a false public sentiment by giving to the world a different code of morals for men and women, by which moral delinquencies which exclude women from society, are not only tolerated but deemed of little account in man.[85]

The Seneca Falls Convention inaugurated first-wave feminism in the United States, formally unleashing centuries of frustration on a society that refused women civic and moral dignity.

Tandem to this practical rebellion was an intellectual revolution spurred on by the relatively new field of analytical psychology. In the early twentieth century, Carl Jung broke away from Sigmund Freud's psychoanalytical theories to develop his own ideas of the individual, self-identity, and an individual's reconciliation with the broader human experience. His various theories on the human psyche, both male and female, resonated within certain spheres of the feminist movement. Jung's concepts gave form to the matter weighing on the hearts of women and the men who sympathized with them. A particular devotee of Jung was Dr. Beatrice Hinkle, an activist and the first female to hold a public health office in the United States. Not only did Hinkle introduce his work to the English-speaking world, but she also harnessed Jungian psychology to consider the roots of feminist malcontent.

[85] Elizabeth Cady Stanton et al., The Declaration of Sentiments (1848), posted on the website of Fordham University, https://sourcebooks.fordham.edu/mod/senecafalls.asp.

In her article "Against the Double Standard," Hinkle likened the women's rights movement to a psychological awakening.[86] She argued that with increased civil liberties and economic independence, women were realizing themselves as distinct beings: substantially, socially, and sexually — especially sexually. Society's moral double standard was the result of men making women "a symbol or personification of man's morality," requiring them to live "for [man] that which he was unable to live for himself" because of the "inferior and inadequate aspect of masculine sexuality that has made it necessary for man to conceive it as something shameful and unclean." Because men were unable, or unwilling, to reckon with their own neuroses, they imposed their masculine morality on the feminine world, repressing woman's identity and agency in society along the way. This imposition, as the Declaration of Sentiments laments, was unjust. The moment women attained economic freedom, it became intolerable: it was man's "youthful ignorance and assurance that the last word has been spoken on this subject that has awakened women, no longer dependent economically, to the fact that they must also become independent of men intellectually if they wish to gain expression for their knowledge or to form their own rules of conduct based on their psychology."

By grounding her argument within the context of disparate sexual moralities between men and women, Hinkle tacitly acknowledged the centrality of sexuality and sexual identity to the feminist movement as a whole. The fight for women's rights was never really about a woman's right to vote, or to have an

---

[86] Dr. Beatrice Hinkle, "Against the Double Standard," posted on the website of Arkansas Tech University, https://faculty.atu.edu/ cbrucker/Engl5383/DoubleStandard.htm.

education, or to enjoy the same sexual freedoms as men: rather, according to Hinkle, it was the fight for women to be free to *be women* in the world, however that is supposed to look, feel, and sound, as men are free to be men in the world. The particular elements of that freedom—voting rights, bodily autonomy, equal access to education and employment opportunities—were the tangible benchmarks by which attainment of that freedom was assessed. In these respects, at least, Hinkle was not wrong;[87] the feminist iterations that followed the suffragette's early efforts were marked by the relentless pursuit of autonomy in personal determination and the legal and moral security to pursue that determination.

It is ironic, then, that the Catholic Church, which advocates for the freedom of the feminine genius to share its gifts with the world, is labeled an enemy of women's dignity and rights. The reverence for the Mother of God, the honor bestowed on female saints and the holy women of Scripture, and all the es-teem that the Church lavishes on women and womanhood are misunderstood, or disregarded, or perverted. A perfect example is St. Birgitta's reputation after her death. The Church saw her as a saint, but others, such as the Swedish playwright August Strindberg, vilified her. In the commentary for his drama *Folkun-gasagan*, he discusses using St. Birgitta as the model for one of his more unsavory characters.: "A domineering, jealous woman who deliberately pursued the sainthood and power over the other sex.... Of this unsympathetic woman, after the records, I made

---

[87] That is, she was not wrong so long as we exclude from the term "bodily autonomy" the modern world's twisted extension of that term to encompass abortion, which destroys the bodily autonomy of babies, some 50 percent of whom are female!

the unruly bitch that is now in the drama, although to her glory I made her awake to the clarity and pride."[88] Unfortunate as it is, this contention is to be expected because the Church and society approach the issues of womanhood and women's dignity and rights from disparate worldviews.

(Un)Natural Opposition

The difference in worldviews between Christian tradition and society reveals itself in the assumptions each side makes about man's prehistoric existence. During the seventeenth and eighteenth centuries, philosophers theorized various primitive states of man and how the introduction of civilized society affected the natural human experience. Some believed in a pre-moral, ignorant-but-innocent state in which man lived in solitary and genteel savagery until the introduction of social contracts. Others believed that man was naturally inclined toward war, with society ordering and inhibiting those tendencies. Still others believed that man's natural state was social but self-interested, with society maintaining balance between the two. But they all held one premise in common: that the human experience is naturally oppositional. And while society at large debated the merits of these social theories, no one questioned the essential premise of man's oppositional nature. Nor would they—this is the way society understands itself. The Enlightenment philosophers were simply furthering a popular social bias.

[88] Ylva Herholz, "Heliga Birgittas Comeback," *Forskning & Framsteg* (April 2003), https://fof.se/tidning/2003/3/heliga-birgittas-comeback.

The Supreme Vocation of Women

This bias is reflected in many of the world's oldest creation myths. In Greek mythology, man was made in the image of the gods, who were killing and eating one another not long before that. The Chinese creation myth has man being formed from parasites feeding off the dead body of Pangu, himself born of a cosmic egg. Similarly, Hindu cosmology believes that society—with its inherent caste systems—originated with the dismemberment and reformation of a cosmic man into the things of the world. And according to ancient Babylon, man was created from the blood of the vanquished god who was responsible for instigating rebellion between the younger and elder gods.

Christian tradition sees the world from a different perspective, which is reflected in the uniqueness of its own creation account in comparison to the others. The Christian worldview holds that man's natural state is one of cooperation. Man is fundamentally good: made to exist in communion, not in conflict. The source of human life is love, not the remains of a dead being or the scavengers that feed off it. Opposition, therefore, is unnatural. It is a later intrusion upon the human experience, brought about by a fatal encounter with evil.

It is worth noting how God fits into each worldview. He is prominent and active in Christian tradition. He is the author of life, giving it form, dignity, and purpose. He is perpetually involved in the work of His creation, and every living thing draws life from Him. Creation reflects the one who created; the higher the creature in the order of the world, the more reflective its nature is of God. And while this reflection is indelible, it is not impervious to damage.

In society's worldview, God is an interloper upon the human experience. At best, He is a remote being with power over the hearts and minds of men: God is the original influencer. At worst, He is a construct of the human conscience: God is man's creation, made to provide external cover for the attempt to make sense of the human experience.

When considering these worldviews, it is important to recognize that by using the distinctions of opposition and cooperation, we are leaning on anthropological constructs. We are evaluating the human experience in humanist terms and basing it on observable patterns of human behavior. If we consider the distinction between worldviews in psychological terms, the conversation moves from the realm of human activity to the realm of human mentality. Optimism and positivity take the place of cooperation, with pessimism and negativity standing in for opposition. And further, in Judeo-Christian religious terms, the distinction between worldviews is rendered thematically: the life of man according to the first two chapters of Genesis versus the life that begins in chapter 4. But regardless of how the distinctions are classified, they all point to the same chasm separating Christian tradition and society: the question of whether the human experience is fundamentally unitive or discordant.

The Making of Medusa

Each worldview produces its own interior logic, by which it governs all other things. Both Christian tradition and society root their logic in the fact of differentiation, the understanding that all things can be distinguished and categorized by traits. They agree that plants are different from animals, and rocks are different from plants; humans and apes share certain characteristics but have distinct and significant differences that place each in discrete categories of mammalia. This is not the cause of their divergent logic. What sets them against each other is the value

that each one places on the notion of difference. That value
is what defines the respective worldviews as either unitive or
discordant. Christian tradition places a positive value on difference. Differences move dependent and independent entities
together toward a whole greater than their selves. They build;
they enhance; they complete; they push forward and upward to a
common end. Society places a negative value on difference. Traditionally, difference is interpreted as an unknown, and anything
unfamiliar is automatically suspect. It is perceived as a potential
threat and treated with prejudice until proven otherwise, or it is
neutralized. Even with the advent of the global community in
the modern era pushing society to reexamine its historical views
on diversity and human value, a tribal mentality pervades social
thought and action.

When it comes to the human experience, there is no more
basic difference than that of male and female. As such, sexuality
has the dubious honor of being the first feature to be assigned a
value. Christian tradition is clear on its judgment of human sexuality: "Male and female he created them.... God saw everything
that he had made, and behold, it was very good" (Gen. 1:27, 31).
This judgment precedes any activity on man or woman's part;
they did not earn their value. Society's judgment on human
sexuality cannot boast the same clarity or objectivity. Without
strict adherence to any single origin story, the human experience
did not have external criteria that would ensure an equitable
judgment upon men and women. There was no person or thing,
above humanity or outside it, to impose a universal standard
upon all people. Instead, society devised its own criteria. Using
the human tools at its disposal—the five senses and rational
ability—these criteria were limited to the temporal world and
the collection of empirical evidence. Value was determined by

function and utility. A thing's "goodness" depended on what it did and how useful it was. This made the process of valuation subjective and mutable, dependent on the prevailing conditions of society at any given time.

Under the utilitarian standards society set for itself, human sexuality was disproportionately valued. Masculinity was caricatured by power and prowess. It set man up as God, as king, as the absolute authority on all things. Femininity was cast as masculinity's foil. It was deemed weak so that man's power had purpose. It was confined to domestic matters so that men could prove their worth in the world. It was labeled lesser, and servile, so that men would always have a nation to rule over. At least, that is what society convinced itself of. Society bought into its oppositional narrative so thoroughly that it became a self-fulfilling prophecy. The sexes moved inexorably toward segregation, with the assumption that men will do what they do, and women will do what they do. Never the two shall meet, except at the dinner table or in the bedroom.

This became the public narrative, the one that history remembers best. It is what the nascent feminist movement rose up against and sought to overthrow. The Seneca Falls Convention accused men of desiring "absolute tyranny" over women, likening the oppression of womanhood to the despotic regimes of Caligula, Fu Sheng, Ivan IV, Oliver Cromwell, and Porfirio Díaz. The only difference, in their minds, was that of duration. These men lasted a few decades, at most, but female repression was systemic, encompassing the whole of human history. Dr. Hinkle validated and furthered their viewpoint in "Against the Double Standard," harnessing feminine disaffection with critical dispassion. She argued that with their increasing focus on sexual mores as a tool of repression, "women are the active agents in the field of sexual morality and men the passive, almost bewildered accessories to the overthrow of their long and firmly organized control of women's sexual conduct." Women, according to Hinkle, were developing a collective "self-consciousness" that refused to tolerate blind obedience to external regulation. They were demanding the freedom to determine the rules that best fit the feminine experience. Women, she continued, wanted their own morality, based on their own psychology and protected under the same rights afforded masculine liberties. They "refuse longer to cater to the traditional notions of them created by men, in which their true feelings and personalities were disregarded and denied."

The Lie of Opposition

In truth, what the feminist movement wanted was the freedom to be as lawless as men. Hinkle herself observed that "women are for the first time demanding to live the forbidden experiences directly ... in the open defiance of [old] customs with feelings of entire justification, or even a non-recognition of a necessity for justification." She also pointed out that "it is easier to break down restrictions than to force them upon those who have hitherto enjoyed comparative freedom." Women were tired of being forced to hold the high ground, with no worldly recompense to show for it, while men rolled in hypocrisy. They wanted the world to be made as much in their image as in the image of man, but rather than identifying and accentuating their own female image, they adopted man's self-determined image. They fought for the right to be powerful, as men were powerful; the right to be sexual, as men were sexual; the right to be autonomous, as men were autonomous. It is debatable whether the early feminists intended to use man's own weapons against him, but by doing so they ensured the perpetuation of the oppositional status quo—albeit under new auspices.

Without any objective perspective on the intrinsic nature and value of the human person, the social issues of our past and our present were bound to happen. Humanity, left to its own devices, is insufficient to master the complexities of the world and its own nature with any consistency or guarantee of accuracy. We are incapable of stepping outside of time to discern the bigger picture because we are too busy moving through it; we are distracted by the details of human living. Society is immersed in the lie that the serpent spun to Eve as truth: "Your eyes will be opened, and you will be like God, knowing good and evil" (Gen. 3:5). We cannot say that he did not warn us.

10

The Power of She Is the Power of We

In her there is a spirit that is intelligent, holy, unique, manifold, subtle, mobile, clear, unpolluted, distinct, invulnerable, loving the good, keen, irresistible, beneficent, humane, steadfast, sure, free from anxiety, all-powerful, overseeing all, and penetrating through all spirits that are intelligent and pure and most subtle. For wisdom is more mobile than any motion; because of her pureness she pervades and penetrates all things. For she is a breath of the power of God, and a pure emanation of the glory of the Almighty; therefore nothing defiled gains entrance into her. For she is a reflection of eternal light, a spotless mirror of the working of God, and an image of his goodness. Though she is but one, she can do all things, and while remaining in herself, she renews all things; in every generation she passes into holy souls and makes them friends of God, and prophets. (Wisd. 7:22–27)

In this passage, the mighty Solomon speaks of wisdom, but his words are equally applicable to womanhood—both of which are known and honored as *she*. Solomon was renowned for his voracious love of wisdom and women, but his downfall came as a result of his inability, or unwillingness, to treat both with the same care and consideration. He collected women, but he received and respected wisdom as a gift of God. Solomon was a hypocritical admirer of the feminine genius, and it cost him his life and the unity of the kingdom. The world accuses the Church of a similar hypocrisy: that she professes a deep, abiding reverence for the dignity and role of women in the life of the Church and in the world yet refuses to allow women to achieve complete operative power in either the Church or the world. It is hard for society to reconcile God's trust in Deborah and Judith to lead armies in defense of His people with a Church that keeps women from the priestly class and visible positions of leadership; strange that the Church affords Mary of Nazareth hyperdulia for her choice to bear the Son of God but bars women from choosing when and how to accept new life in relation to their own. The Church, in refusing to let women do things like these, appears to the world as if she is forfeiting her own life by suppressing the agency of half of her members and tearing her own kingdom apart from the inside with her narrow-minded hubris.

But what the world fails to take into account is that the Church does not conceive of herself as an *it*, but as a *she*. The Church is a living entity, made for union and communion with Christ and with others. Her feminine identity "is of *fundamental importance for understanding the Church in her* own *essence*, so as to avoid applying to the Church ... criteria of understanding and judgment which do not pertain to her nature."[89]

---

[89] *Mulieris Dignitatem*, no. 27.

The Origin of *She*

In the Old Testament, the people of God believed in and awaited the kingdom of God. Their conception of this kingdom, and how they perceived their unification within it, was overtly hierarchal and masculine in tone. God (*He*) would reign over all, with the cooperation of an anointed earthly king (another *he*) and a priestly class (all *he*) to guide the people. This was the ideal, the promise that encouraged generations of faithful to have hope in the midst of slavery and suffering. When the events of the Gospels unfolded, the coming kingdom of God was still the hope of the people, and the Messiah was eagerly anticipated. As the Messiah and His kingdom revealed themselves, however, it was not what the Hebrew people expected. The promised king was not a king under God but claimed to be the Son of God. His kingdom was not won by the blood of His enemies but by His own blood. As for the kingdom itself, it was not a territory defined by walls and defended by armies. Instead, it was a community of persons bound by love and infused with grace. The kingdom was not established but born — emerging from the Messiah as a body enlivened with the Spirit of God.

In the Acts of the Apostles, the nascent Christian community begins to formulate its identity under the leadership of St. Peter and the apostles and a new addition to the fold: Saul of Tarsus, better known as St. Paul. Much of their energies are devoted to establishing temporal order to the community, in imitation and continuation of the fellowship that Christ established with His Twelve. Though the male hierarchy is retained, and the priestly class is set apart, as it was in the Hebrew tradition, both are imbued with the same subtle shift in perspective that made it difficult for the Hebrew people to see the fulfillment of Scripture in the person of Jesus Christ. St. Paul, especially, speaks to this new perspective that Christ imparted to all things. In his First Letter to the Corinthians, St. Paul likens the nature of the Christian community to a body: Christ is the Head, and every believer is a part of the body and works in cooperation with the other parts and under the guidance of the Head as a unified whole. Unlike a kingdom, which stratifies its subjects, a body holds all of its parts in esteem: "The eye cannot say to the hand, 'I have no need of you,' nor again the head to the feet, 'I have no need of you.' ... But God has so adjusted the body, giving the greater honor to the inferior part, that there may be no discord in the body, but that the members may have the same care for one another. If one member suffers, all suffer together; if one member is honored, all rejoice together" (1 Cor. 12:21, 24–26). Later, in his Letter to the Ephesians, St. Paul extends his body metaphor further, likening the community to a *female* body—the Bride to Christ the Bridegroom. He says:

> Be subject to one another out of reverence for Christ. Wives, be subject to your husbands, as to the Lord. For the husband is the head of the wife as Christ is the head of the church, his body, and is himself its Savior. As the church is subject to Christ, so let wives also be subject in everything to their husbands. Husbands, love your wives, as Christ loved the church and gave himself up for her, that he might sanctify her, having cleansed her by the washing of water with the word, that he might present the church to himself in splendor, without spot or wrinkle or any such thing, that she might be holy and without blemish. Even so husbands should love their wives as their own bodies. He who loves his wife loves himself. For no man ever hates his own flesh, but nourishes and cherishes

it, as Christ does the church, because we are members of his body. (Eph. 5:21–30)

The nuptial analogy struck a chord with the faithful as no other had done before. It recognized and manifested a particular truth about the nature of the Christian community—namely, its humanity. The Church, as *she*, is endowed with personhood. She is not a construct or an object, a thing to be possessed or fought over or bartered. This personality extends to her agency: her operative power comes from her capacity to be in communion with Christ, her spouse. As *she*, the Church is Christ's cooperative partner in the work of salvation, receiving His unending love and grace and extending it to the whole world.

"Be Subject to One Another"

St. Paul's nuptial analogy is often misconstrued as an overt defense of the hierarchal dominance of men over women and a root of women's devaluation in Christian tradition, but that is a superficial and incomplete reading of St. Paul's message. Rather, in keeping with Christ's radical words and way of treating women, the analogy furthers the dignity of the feminine experience and encourages a broader understanding of its practical wisdom within the whole of the human experience. St. Paul opens with the clear summation, "Be subject to one another out of reverence for Christ." He speaks to men and women without distinction, making a single qualification: their mutual subjection to the other must flow from a unified subjection to Christ. The subjection of the wife to her husband, like that of the Church to Christ, is not an act of enslavement to an impersonal king but an act of love that responds to the gift of her beloved. It completes and perpetuates the cycle of communion between persons. Similarly, the subjection of the husband as the "head" of his wife, in imitation of Christ as Head of the Church, initiates the cycle of communion; the Bridegroom invites the Bride into a relationship of reciprocal giving by offering Himself up for her and asking her to return His love. This kind of invitation requires a deep humility on the part of the initiator; he must be open to the lived experience of another, taking it upon himself as if the experience were his own. Openness to others is already ingrained in the feminine reality, which explains St. Paul's brevity when speaking to wives about the nature of their role. But the fact that he makes a protracted explanation of the nature of the husband's role indicates that the nuptial analogy is intended to reorient the masculine experience toward a closer alignment with the feminine experience, rather than extol the former's superiority over the latter. St. Paul is preparing all disciples, but especially men, "to respond—as a bride—with the gift of their lives to the inexpressible gift of the love of Christ, who alone, as the Redeemer of the world, is the Church's Bridegroom."[90]

The Dimensions of Response

The bridal response of the Church is to share in the life of her Spouse, uniting her life to His. This is expressed through the dimensions of the universal, royal priesthood and the particular, ministerial priesthood. All baptized persons participate in the universal priesthood, taking up holiness as their mission and the Mother of God as their model. The ministerial priesthood is reserved for men who, like Peter and the apostles, are specifically

[90] *Mulieris Dignitatem*, no. 27.

called by Christ to unite themselves in a more complete way to His threefold mission as priest, prophet, and king. Despite the exclusivity of the apostolic hierarchy, the Church holds that the apostolic dimension is "totally ordered to the holiness of Christ's members":

> This Marian profile is also — even perhaps more so — fundamental and characteristic for the Church as is the apostolic and Petrine profile to which it is profoundly united.... The Marian dimension of the Church is antecedent to that of the Petrine, without being in any way divided from it or being less complementary. Mary Immaculate precedes all others, including obviously Peter himself and the Apostles. This is so, not only because Peter and the Apostles, being born of the human race under the burden of sin, form part of the Church which is "holy from out of sinners," but also because their triple function has no other purpose except to form the Church in line with the ideal of sanctity already programmed and prefigured in Mary. A contemporary theologian has rightly stated that Mary is "Queen of the Apostles without any pretensions to apostolic powers: she has other and greater powers."[91]

In a sense, this echoes the nuptial analogy, with the ministerial priesthood taking the place of the husband and the universal priesthood taking the place of the wife. Both are subject to Christ, and each is subject to the other. The ministerial priesthood, *in persona Christi*, extends an invitation to the beloved faithful (and to themselves), drawing all to intimate union with

[91] Ibid., quoting Hans Urs von Balthasar, *Neue Klarstellungen*.

Christ through the sacraments, prayer, and the cultivation of virtue. Like a good husband, the ministerial priesthood submits his authority to the service and sanctification of others, so that they may be "holy and without blemish." And in return, the universal priesthood responds with her own Marian fiat: submitting herself to the grace of the sacraments, lifting her voice in prayers of the Mass and in private prayer, and embracing the wisdom of a moral life.

"Other and Greater Powers"

It is common knowledge that the Petrine dimension of the Church holds the power and the authority to interpret and teach the truth of divine revelation and all that rightly flows from it. It binds the Church in her catholicity, making her truly one body that operates with the mind and the spirit of Christ, her Head. This power is a great and visible one; a sight to behold, whether it comes from the foot of the altar or the bishop's desk. The Marian dimension does not appear to have a similar visibility or a corresponding authority. Indeed, it does not, because this kind of response is not called to the same thing—it is not called to a thing at all but to a person. The royal priesthood is invited to unite herself to *the person* of Christ. She is offered the opportunity to share His very being: His body and blood, His breath, His warmth, His joy, His sorrow, His thoughts, His desires. Those in the ministerial priesthood are called to unite themselves to Christ's *office*, His singular work of redemption. This work is grand and visible, exercised with authority and requiring spectacular sacrifice. But it *follows* unity with the person of Christ. A ministerial priest must first be a universal priest.

In this way the universal-royal priesthood, the nuptial analogy, and the Church's identity as *she* lead us back to the familiar conclusion that the efficacious power and agency of the feminine experience is in her capacity to bring the human experience into a state of communion: communion between persons and the communion of all persons with God. *She* "passes through holy souls and makes them friends of God, and prophets" (Wisd. 7:27). Womanhood leads the royal priesthood in the pursuit of holiness. Her power and authority come from her capacity to develop the human person in his or her fullness, to bring light to all that is good and true about the human experience, which ultimately reflects the goodness and truth of God. *She* is able to hold the gaze of God and say, "I am the handmaid of the Lord; let it be to me according to your word" (Luke 1:38). And leveling her gaze at the world, with the same breath she is unafraid to command, "Do whatever he tells you" (John 2:5).

Note from a Sentinel

Dear Reader,

A lifetime ago, I had a spirited conversation with a young woman about the Church and her views on women. At the end, she told me I should write a book on the subject—that maybe, if more people saw the Church the way I did, fewer would leave the Faith. I vowed to her that I would, enamored with the idea that I might be able to do something good for the Church. I was young, and a recent convert to boot; that kind of naïve optimism knows no bounds. Life got in the way, and I forgot my vow. She probably did as well. But God did not. When the time was right, He reminded me. Everything fell into place for me to make good on my promise, if I was still willing to honor it. Obviously I was, and here we are. My hope is that you come away with a better understanding of what the Church holds true about the human person, and women in particular.

The truth is, in the eyes of the Church, Ellen Ripley and June Cleaver[92] are essentially the same woman. I grew up surrounded

---

[92] The main character in the *Alien* movies and the mother in the 1950s sitcom *Leave It to Beaver*, respectively.

by women who were as comfortable roasting a chicken as they were confronting the evils of the world; the image of a woman wearing an apron with a metaphorical blowtorch in her back pocket seemed not only plausible but normative. And the Church affirms this, without equivocation. In Scripture, she is Judith, and she is Mary. In Tradition, she is St. Birgitta and St. Monica and St. Elizabeth and hundreds of others. Only, unless you are specifically looking for it, this affirmation is easily overlooked. In a way, the Church assumed female dignity and agency much as I did in my early years, because the reality of it surrounds our whole lived experience. It was like breathing: so familiar as to be unremarkable.

Until it wasn't anymore. The apparent novelty of John Paul II's papal writings is an indictment of how long the Church allowed herself to operate on autopilot with this aspect of the Faith. The Polish pope did not revolutionize Church teaching. In fact, he was rigorous in his continuity with Scripture and Tradition. That should be obvious to every one of us, but it isn't. No matter how you view the legacy of John Paul II, he gave us a great gift. He offered a fresh way to understand and explain the eternal truths of the human person and how vital womanhood is to the proclamation of those truths. He presented the Faith in more robust language and offered an explicit invitation for all of us to come together and renew our understanding of the fundamental elements that make up human society. He enabled us to look back at the Church Fathers and the medieval scholars and discern the catholicity of their message within their particular times.

If you've never read John Paul II's works, I strongly recommend that you do so. If you have, read more of them. Or go back and reread what you are familiar with. Sit with his words awhile.

They will challenge you to reflect on what you believe and why you hold such beliefs. It won't be easy, but it will be edifying.

John Paul II's provocative appeal for women to be *sentinels of the Invisible* is an essential part of his gift. It is also a great challenge; more than a call to action, it is a call to *identity*. We can't be content with what we already think we know about womanhood—there is more to her than we are giving her credit for. And our ignorance, Catholic and non-Catholic alike, is hurting the whole human experience.

For instance, John Paul II's idea of the feminine genius is further elucidated by the qualities of receptivity, sensitivity, generosity, and maternity. These qualities have become the de facto terms associated with the feminine genius in the minds of the faithful. John Paul II didn't use these qualities to define the feminine genius, however. In fact, he never attributed a clear definition to his idea of the feminine genius.

Receptivity, sensitivity, generosity, and maternity are the main qualities that Mary Jo Anderson articulated[93] to synthesize the message in *Mulieris Dignitatem*, and they just happened to catch fire. The problem with this is that emphasizing these qualities as particular to the *female* genius insinuates that the *male* genius is bereft of them. Men can't be, or struggle to be, receptive, sensitive, and generous? I have a father, a husband, three sons, two uncles, a small army of brothers-in-law, and a large number of male friends who have those qualities in spades, disproving the blanket claim of "can't." Arguing that men struggle to be receptive, sensitive, and generous may have

---

[93] Mary Jo Anderson, "Feminine Genius," *Catholic Answers*, July 1, 2005, https://www.catholic.com/magazine/print-edition/feminine-genius.

more merit, but that is not a deficit of nature. That is cultural conditioning. It is the perpetuation of sexist stereotypes. I have no doubt that Ms. Anderson came up with these without malice. She, like many women, only want womanhood to be duly recognized for its good gifts. But it reveals how ingrained social stigmas are in the human consciousness and how they affect us without our realizing it.

Maybe understanding women as *sentinels of the Invisible* will be the key to liberating the human experience from stereotype and prejudice. Taking us back "to the beginning," it enables us to orient womanhood in the cosmic order of things, which automatically orients the whole of human sexuality. In a sense, it gives us the opportunity to wipe the slate clean, to toss out the ignorant and misguided tropes and cultivate a sense of the sexes that authentically reflects and celebrates the dignity of each. But, to do this, we must value the human person as God does, not as we have come to value ourselves. God created complementary distinction, not isolating differences; we have no one to blame but ourselves for the existence of prejudice and discrimination. And this brings us to the crux of the challenge that being a *sentinel of the Invisible* presents: How willing are we to let God define us? How willing are we to let go of our own social constructs and follow where the logic of the Lord takes us? More to the point, what is our worldview? What do we take as our starting point while we navigate and evaluate our human experience?

I don't know what worldview you had at the start of this book, but I hope you know that where you go from here matters. You and I have the opportunity to do some real good for each other and for future generations. Nothing we do is insignificant, and nothing is wasted. Everything we say and everything we do, and how we say and do these things, pushes the world in one direction or another. Let's be sure of what direction our lives are pushing toward.

In Christ,
Melissa

About the Author

Melissa Maleski is a speaker, writer, and director of youth and young adult ministry. She regularly presents at faith-formation conferences and parish retreats and consults on special diocesan initiatives. Melissa has also served as a catechist and director of religious education. Her early work was featured in *Homiletic and Pastoral Review*, and she has collaborated on a number of catechetical materials for youth and families. A young-adult convert, she earned a master of arts in theological studies from Christendom College's Graduate School in 2015. Melissa shares her many adventures with her husband and four children.

Sophia Institute

Sophia Institute is a nonprofit institution that seeks to nurture the spiritual, moral, and cultural life of souls and to spread the gospel of Christ in conformity with the authentic teachings of the Roman Catholic Church.

Sophia Institute Press fulfills this mission by offering translations, reprints, and new publications that afford readers a rich source of the enduring wisdom of mankind.

Sophia Institute also operates the popular online resource CatholicExchange.com. *Catholic Exchange* provides world news from a Catholic perspective as well as daily devotionals and articles that will help readers to grow in holiness and live a life consistent with the teachings of the Church.

In 2013, Sophia Institute launched Sophia Institute for Teachers to renew and rebuild Catholic culture through service to Catholic education. With the goal of nurturing the spiritual, moral, and cultural life of souls, and an abiding respect for the role and work of teachers, we strive to provide materials and programs that are at once enlightening to the mind and ennobling to the heart; faithful and complete, as well as useful and practical.

Sophia Institute gratefully recognizes the Solidarity Association for preserving and encouraging the growth of our apostolate over the course of many years. Without their generous and timely support, this book would not be in your hands.

www.SophiaInstitute.com
www.CatholicExchange.com
www.SophiaInstituteforTeachers.org

Sophia Institute Press® is a registered trademark of Sophia Institute.
Sophia Institute is a tax-exempt institution as defined by the Internal Revenue Code, Section 501(c)(3). Tax ID 22-2548708.